DIGITAL TEXTILE DESIGN

MELANIE BOWLES AND CERI ISAAC

LAURENCE KING PUBLISHING

CONTENTS:

INTRODUCTION

Digital technology is changing the face of textile design, from methods of creating and presenting designs to the ways in which they are realized. Working in a digital environment, designers are afforded more time to experiment, explore and create, while manufacturing technologies offer innovative new printing solutions. This practical and inspirational book examines a new era of textile design and features clear tutorials and case studies revealing how digital techniques are being employed in the fashion-, interior design- and home furnishings industries.

The development of digital printing onto fabric is changing printing methods and removing the restrictions that textile designers have traditionally faced: freed from concerns about repeat patterns and colour separation that are key considerations in screen- and roller printing, designers are able to work with thousands of colours and create designs with a high level of detail. There is also greater freedom for experimentation, facilitating one-off production as well as smaller print runs and prints engineered specifically to fit the form of a garment.

Software programs such as Adobe Photoshop and Illustrator present the perfect platform for textile design. These have become the industry standard tools for textile designers, offering them the freedom to work with both bitmap and vector-based imagery, manipulate drawings and photographs, and create accurate details and graphic effects.

While digital printing allows a rich mix of layered imagery, the surface and tactile qualities associated with some methods of traditional printing can be lost: as a result designers are finding ways to put these qualities back into the fabric using techniques such as overprinting and embellishment, and this combination of digital and handcrafted techniques has even created a new hybrid craft.

Whatever your interest in textiles – whether you are a student or professional, designer or producer – you will find this to be an essential and comprehensive guide to an exciting new field that is pushing the boundaries of textile design.

CHAPTER 1
TEXTILE DESIGN
AND PRINT IN
THE DIGITAL AGE

NEW DIRECTIONS IN TEXTILE DESIGN

As the most significant advance in fabric-printing technology since the invention of the silk screen, digital textile printing is bringing about a revolution in textile design. Designers are seeking inspiration from previously unexplored sources, and a new visual language for surface design is starting to evolve.

The cross-disciplinary use of graphics software, digital photography, video and special effects by a hybrid generation of young designers is creating a new look for printed fabrics. Fashion designers such as Issey Miyake, Hussein Chalayan and Comme des Garçons are breaking new ground with the creation and use of highly innovative prints that make little reference to traditional patterns: florals have been reinvented through the use of photography, and geometric designs as the focal point of a garment have been given a futuristic edge by designers such as Jonathan Saunders. There is also more scope for the use of large, engineered or placement prints where the artwork is tailored to fit the structure of the garment. Designers working in other areas such as costume-, theatre-, interior- and product design are also finding it easier to involve themselves in the creation of surface designs for their work. The accessibility of this technology through the use of service bureaus also makes it possible for artists and designers who do not have specialist knowledge of textile printing to design and produce their own fabrics and decorative surfaces.

The use of digital print is relatively new and, due to its high cost, is only really feasible at the high- and middle ends of the fashion and textile design industry (as demonstrated by the range of examples shown in this chapter). But already it is drawing together disciplines such as textiles, fashion and interior design, changing the way that designers work. Increasingly, the integration of print is becoming as vital to the designer's vision as the form of the garment or product itself due to the immediacy and spontaneity of digital tools.

This chapter looks at the impact of this new technology on textile design and explores the work of both well-known and emerging designers who are using computer-aided design and digital print to their full potential throughout a wide range of applications.

From top to bottom:
Danish designer and Central Saint Martins graduate Dorte Agergaard Jensen places everyday objects in unusual contexts, as seen in her range of printed bed linen.
Surface designer Helena Britt has used digital printing to create a distinctive collection of interior products, printing on materials ranging from canvas to leather.
This Paul Smith bag is digitally printed with trompe l'oeil football designs, and features the ubiquitous Paul Smith stripes.

Clockwise from left:
Sarah Arnett, 'Betty' ready-to-wear collection
S/S 08; digital print on silk georgette.
Basso & Brooke, S/S 08: ambassadors of digital
print, the designers have departed from their
signature graphic style with this painterly dress.
Sarah Easom, S/S 09: colourful graphic floral-
printed gown with pleated skirt.
Cloth: custom-printed chair by this UK-based
digital print and design company demonstrates
how any product can be personalized.

DIGITAL TEXTILE PRINTING

The digital printing of textiles grew out of reprographic technologies originally developed for paper- and signage printing, and it now offers the same advantages to the textile industry that digital production affords the paper- and banner printing businesses. For individual designers and hobbyists it is analogous to the rise of desktop publishing, albeit more costly. The reason why the technology has been slower to emerge in the textile industry was because of the need to develop suitable inks and large-format printers specifically designed to accommodate woven as well as stretchable cloth. The emergence of large-format digital-textile printers, such as the Mimaki in 1998, and then the release of industrial-scale printers in 2003 by companies such as Konica, Minolta, Reggiani, Robustelli and Dupont, means that there is now the potential for major changes in the textile and fashion industries in terms of increased speed and long-run capability. The introduction of the ISIS printer by OSIRIS in 2008 may even mean that the speed of inkjet printing machines may begin to rival that of traditional rotary screen printing.

Digital printing has perhaps four main advantages over traditional print: speed of translation of the design onto the fabric; the ability to print intricate details and millions of colours; the possibility of producing very large-scale images; lessened impact on the environment. Traditional methods of printing based on processes similar to stencilling – including silk screen, woodblock and gravure – first require that a separate template for each colour be made, and for the image to then be built up in stages as each colour must be laid down separately. The more colours, the more expensive and time-consuming the process, so that the number of colours is limited by practical considerations, often placing considerable restraints upon the designer. Repeated patterns are the norm in industrialized traditional textile printing, and very large-scale images are also impractical as the size of the design is constrained to the exact measurements of the template.

Digital printing means that there is virtually no limit to the kinds of images that may accurately be reproduced using inkjet technology. It is this exciting advantage that has paved the way for the new styles of design that are explored in this chapter.

From top to bottom:
Jonathan Saunders' minimalist prints blend into the undecorated parts of this garment through the use of solid colours that match elements of the print design.
Giles Deacon's bold print shows how digital tools may be used to create special effects through the abstraction of an image.
This carefully constructed print by Basso & Brooke illustrates two main advantages of digital print: it allows the use of a large number of colours, and it enables the designer to engineer the print to the form of the body. It would be possible to print this using traditional methods, but preparing a template for each colour would be time-consuming and costly.

Ambassadors of élite fashion, couturiers Jean Paul Gaultier (left) and Ralph Rucci (below) use digitally designed and printed fabrics as a device for the embellishment of their creations. Although the prints in both of these evening gowns are subtle in terms of colour and imagery, they are the focal points of the garments. Gaultier has added a level of mystery to his gown, drawing the viewer's eye into the textures and patterns formed by a digitally-manipulated photograph of the frayed pages of antique books.
Rucci has used striated patterns, as found in the semiprecious gem malachite, in his garment, perhaps to emphasize the idea that it is also a work of art.

A NEW VISUAL LANGUAGE

Historically, the introduction of new technology does not usually result in an immediate change in design styles. Initially, design for any industrial application continues to follow the style associated with the preceding technology; the first motorcars, for example, were designed to resemble horse-drawn carriages. Change only begins to occur once practitioners come to understand the potential of a new technology and are comfortable with it.

Heat-transfer printing aside, the introduction of inkjet printing for textiles has meant that textile designers are now able to catch up with graphic designers by exploring the possibilities of computer-aided design (CAD). The early design styles that resulted from the introduction of digital imaging were often obviously computer-generated; the focus was on displaying technology for its own sake rather than using CAD as a tool for achieving a more sophisticated visual effect. A more mature style of digital textile design is now evolving due to increased experimentation by designers, who are creating designs based on scanned or digitally photographed subjects, facilitating effects such as trompe l'oeil as well as graphic and illustrative styles that are only possible using computerized drawing and manipulation tools. Designers are also beginning to combine digital print with traditional techniques to create a new digital craft, which is explored in Chapter Five.

DIGITAL SURFACE DESIGN AND PHOTOGRAPHY

The use of photography first became noticeable in textile design in the 1960s and 70s, when dye-sublimation (or heat-transfer) printing onto synthetic high-polymer content fabrics such as polyester first became prevalent. As software packages that could manipulate imagery, such as Adobe Photoshop, were not yet available, designs tended to be based on photomontage or collage, such as the ubiquitous 'disco' shirts of the 1970s.

Being able to manipulate and transform an image digitally means that incorporating photography into textile design is now much more sympathetic to the nature of cloth as a material. Cloth comes to life in a way that paper does not: it moves, reflects light, and is often transparent or highly textured. Photographs formatted as if for printing onto paper can make a stark and incongruous statement when translated onto fabric. Designing a textile often involves a very different sensibility from that inherent in pure photography. On paper, photographs are usually intended as narrative documents, whereas the hybrid use of photography in textile design has begun to create a very different style in which the image is subtle or abstracted.

Nicolette Brunklaus is a Dutch designer who makes very clever use of digital print in her range of home furnishings. This hugely enlarged photograph of cascading blonde hair is used as wallpaper that is somehow oddly reminiscent of landscape wallpaper of the 1960s and 1970s.

Paul Smith is a pioneer of digital surface design, using inkjet prints in both his menswear and womenswear collections. The majority of his digital textile designs are photographic in style, such as this daffodil-print dress.

Showroom Dummies, a group of British designers headed by Abigail Lane, uses digital imaging as the focal point for its work. This British company produces an eclectic range of products that spans home furnishings and clothing. Their signature print, shown here, of clouds and flies against a blue sky is both surreal and humorous.

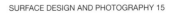

Above: This design is a collaboration between Ceri Isaac and Hitoshi Ujiie. An object was specially created and photographed, and then the motif was isolated, abstracted and layered transparently to form the design.

Left: Ceri Isaac's work uses photographs or textures reminiscent of traditional patterns that are not too obviously computer generated. This pattern of birds in flight was made by taking motion stills from video footage by Martin Stumph and collaging selected areas together in Photoshop. The colours were also enhanced in Photoshop.

GRAPHIC AND ILLUSTRATIVE STYLES

As the generation that has come of age in the digital era, many young and emerging textile designers have begun to use digital prints in their collections. For some it provides a natural foundation for the conceptualization of their work, and they seamlessly integrate their other design skills as graphic and illustrative artists into the creation of each piece of work.

Win Sei Yau's playful and colourful cartoon-style prints are what set her graduate collection at the London College of Fashion apart.

Hussein Chalayan printed this gown with an image reminiscent of an Old Master painting. It would not be possible to reproduce the exquisite detail and millions of colours using traditional silk-screen methods.

Timorous Beasties' designs reference traditional pattern, while remaining truly modern. Paying homage to the toile, they created a beautifully drawn Glasgow skyline that illustrates local life. Here they show how hand-drawing and skilled draftsmanship may coexist alongside digital tools.

Lucinda Abell's talent as an illustrator is apparent in the beautifully drafted fairytale images and intricate floral designs she created for her graduation fashion collection.

Trompe l'oeil, a French expression that translates as 'trick of the eye', is used to describe extremely realistic imagery created to give the illusion that the depicted objects really exist, instead of being what they really are – a two-dimensional image. This is a style that lends itself especially well to digital design.

For this 'hair cut' shirt, created for her MA collection, London College of Fashion graduate Jula Reindell plays with our perception of a two-dimensional surface.

Comme des Garçons use trompe l'oeil to full effect through the conceptualization of a garment and its draping on the body, by printing a full-scale image of a dress on a dress. The image has been carefully engineered from a photograph to appear almost as though it has been projected onto the model.

Chelsea College of Art and Design graduate Chae Young Kim created this trompe l'oeil-effect by superimposing an interior space onto a garment.

DESIGN ADVANTAGES

As we have already touched upon, digital textile printing has some major advantages over traditional printing methods in design terms. These are: immediacy; the ability to print intricate details and millions of colours as well the possibility of printing images on a much larger scale; being able to create customized products and engineered designs.

The immediacy of digital tools in the rapid transformation of ideas into finished garments is crucial in the high-speed word of fashion. Experimentation and the evolution of a concept through a process of trial and error is an essential part of the creative process, and digital print is the perfect tool to facilitate this.

Prior to the introduction of inkjet textile printing, with the exception of heat-transfer printing onto polyester-based fabrics, it was not possible to translate the millions of colours required to reproduce all the nuances of images such as oil paintings, watercolours or photographs onto natural-fibre fabrics. Printers such as the Mimaki TX2 are capable of printing much finer lines than is possible using traditional rotary screens (see Chapter Six), and millions of colours may be used in a single image.

In addition to the design advantages offered by digital printing, inkjet textile printing is significantly more eco-friendly than traditional rotary- and flatbed silk-screen methods. According to some estimates, digital printers consume fifty percent less energy than traditional rotary screen printing machines. There is also less wastage of materials as less dye or pigment is used in laying down the image than in traditional industrial methods, and water is saved as there are no screens to wash.

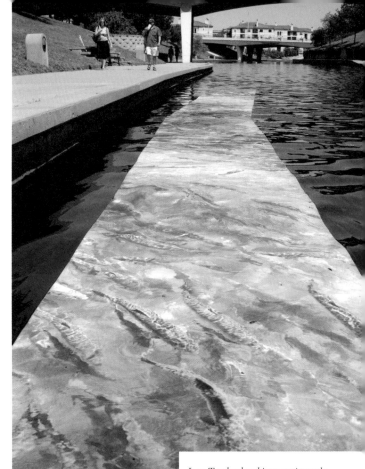

Joan Truckenbrod is an artist at the Art Institute of Chicago who has been creating computer-generated images since the 1970s. She was among the first artists to explore digital fabric printing as a fine art form. Here, her digitally printed image of swimming fish was floated in Brush Creek, Kansas City.

LARGE-SCALE PRINTS

With traditional printing techniques, repeats were constrained to the size of the pattern block, the size of the screen or the circumference of the roller, thus limiting the scale of the pattern. By eliminating the screen, digital print has transformed textile design, and the designer's decision to use a repeated pattern is an aesthetic choice rather than a technical necessity.

The use of digital tools such as Photoshop and Illustrator in conjunction with the ability to print on a larger scale makes it easier to create designs that fit the pattern piece for a garment exactly. Such designs are know as 'engineered' or 'placement' prints. All the pattern pieces containing the print may then be grouped together as 'a lay plan' that is ready to cut and sew. This technique can also be taken one step further into the realm of custom design.

These huge textile panels are the canvas for Heather Ujiie's delicate illustrations. Heather combines hand- and digital drawing, initially sketching and refining the imagery by hand before scanning it and redrawing it in Illustrator. She applies to her digital work the skills she acquired in painting intricate croquis for the traditional textile market.

LAY PLANS

In his A/W 07/08 collection, Hussein Chalayan experimented with scanning and digitally manipulating fabrics used in his ready-to-wear collection, creating a trompe l'oeil effect, capturing the textures of the weave. Once these textures and patterns were digitized, they were overlaid as transparent layers and laid out as geometric shapes within the engineered pattern pieces, creating an unusual harmony.

Chalayan's prints are emblematic of his overall ability to fascinate by removing what has inspired him from its original context and then reconstructing something new. The image below shows the lay plan containing the printed pattern pieces used to create the garments seen on the catwalk, right.

ENGINEERED PRINTS

Historically, the apparel and footwear industries have moved from handmade customized clothing, through to the industrialized mass-production of generically standardized fitted clothing, and onto digitally-tailored clothing.

An 'engineered', or 'placement' print, is tailored to fit the pattern pieces of a garment in such a way that, when assembled, there is a degree of continuity – the design flows unbroken around the body and the image or repeated pattern is not broken by the seams. Notable designers of the twentieth century such as Sonia Delaunay, Emilio Pucci and Gianni Versace favoured engineered screen printing. These garments are perceived as being more luxurious if a placement print were employed, as such designs are more costly and time-consuming to produce. Recently Tristan Webber, Jonathan Saunders, Basso & Brooke and Alexander McQueen have all employed the technique using digital textile printing.

The fact that digital tools make it easier to create an engineered print is a very exciting prospect for fashion- and textile designers alike, as both digital print and digitally-fitted garments can be brought together. Designers have used geometric designs that follow the form of the body to enhance the sculptural effects of a garment's cut. Engineered prints may also be used more subtly to highlight elements such as cuffs, collars and bodices.

This Alexander McQueen dress has been carefully engineered so that the differently coloured bands of overlapping feathers circle the waist and then spread out to fit the skirt as it widens.

LARGE- AND SMALL-SCALE CUSTOMIZATION

Digital printing is ideally suited to the creation of limited-edition designs that are customized to suit the tastes of an individual client. The addition of body scanning, as well as the introduction of software that automatically generates pattern pieces based on the scanned data, streamlines the process of placing a printed design exactly within a garment.

A body scanner digitally captures 3D measurements to create a virtual model of an individual's body. This not only means that a tape measure is no longer necessary when fitting a client, but that many more measurements are taken than would be practical when performing a fitting by hand. Department stores such as Selfridges and Harrods in London now provide this service.

While digital printing can be used to make one-off fitted designs, the technology can also be used for mass customization. Companies such as Nike use the Internet as a vehicle for mass customization, providing customers with the ability to individualize and 'build' a product by allowing them to choose certain options. If the choices are limited to certain colours and design elements then the result will not be unique. Whereas companies such as Cloth do construct one-of-a-kind pieces of upholstered furniture by digitally printing an image sent to them by the client.

Austrian company Wexla have a modular shoe system that allows for both mass customization as well as a personalized product. Customers choose from a variety of shoe bases and uppers and may even upload their own image to be printed.

This footstool by Cloth has been personalized with the customer's photographs.

CUSTOMIZED JEANS

For its centenary celebration in 2006/2007, researchers at the London College of Fashion collaborated to explore how state-of-the-art technology could be used to create a one-of-a-kind garment. The idea was to design one-off fitted and digitally printed jeans, and the project would integrate 3D body scanning, automatic pattern generation, digital printing and digital embroidery. The project explored how the technology could be used to streamline the process of engineering the print onto the garment as well as testing the accuracy of matching an image across the seams.

Image of the Manhattan skyline (above) by Ceri Isaac printed on to jeans and (right) the lay plan showing the pattern pieces.

Above: specialist software enables the embroidered areas to match up with the printed design.

Left: still from an animated virtual catwalk. This digital 'try-on' software meant that the concept for the jeans could be tested on an avatar before the design was finalized.

FASTER PRINT TIMESCALES

The fashion world moves at an extremely fast pace, and designers such as Paul Smith now have the added pressure of creating two collections for every season. Originality is crucial and it is hardly surprising that top designers are increasingly attracted to the possibilities that new technology has to offer in generating ideas for their collections. Digital design and printing are the perfect tools for high-speed fashion, as it is possible to deliver ready-to-wear fabric the same day, depending on the quantity required.

The speed with which fabric may be produced, together with the accessibility of design technology, is closing the gap between the textile design industry and its clients – the fashion- and interior designers. In the West, the making of most printed and decorative textiles was historically the domain of specialist master craftsmen, their expertise acquired through many years of practice and apprenticeship. The textile and tailoring trades, although entirely dependent upon each other, were seen as separate professions. In catering for their wealthier clients, some designers would have commissioned special fabrics to suit their whims, but, for the most part, printed fabrics were bought from merchants stocking standard types of cloth. Digital print technology is changing this.

LOOKING TO THE FUTURE

A degree of separation between textile design and fashion is still the norm today. The current system of textile production supports the mass consumption of cheap goods and so reinforces the distance between the fashion- and textile designer. Also, as fashion designers generally have higher profiles than textile designers, textile designers are sadly rarely credited alongside the name of the fashion designer who has used their design.

At the higher end of the market, digital design and printing is rapidly closing the gap between textiles and fashion. If this trend continues, it will inevitably make its way down to the mid- and lower end of the market. Digital textile printing technology is advancing rapidly and has the potential to aid the creation of higher quality goods. It may be hoped that, as digital design blurs the boundaries between professions such as fashion, textiles and interior design, the consumer will come to value quality rather than quantity, and so move away from throw-away fashion and its harmful effect on the environment.

SPONTANEOUS FASHION

British designer Hussein Chalayan has used digital print to great effect in many of his collections. Since his graduate collection, when he began to experiment with garments that move independently of the body, his name has become synonymous with the emerging digital print technology.

The print for this dress from his S/S 07 '1011' collection is not quite what it first appears. The design evolved from a photograph that one of Chalayan's assistants took of the mannequin and toile for the dress while documenting the design process. Chalayan and his team saw the potential to create a print from the slightly surreal imagery.

The figure in the photograph was isolated from its background, subtly recoloured in Photoshop, then put into repeat, before being digitally printed. Viewed from a distance, the print resembles a traditional floral design, but when viewed closer up it reveals itself to be an entirely different motif. This is an excellent example of the immediacy that digital printing affords.

Close-up detail of the image that has been printed onto the finished fabric. An example of how the fast turnaround enabled by digital printing is transforming design methods.

CHAPTER 2
DIGITAL DESIGN
TUTORIALS

INTRODUCTION

Adobe Photoshop and Illustrator together offer a perfect platform for textile design. While the bitmap-based Photoshop gives you the freedom to edit and manipulate drawings and photographs, the vector-based Illustrator enables the creation of accurate graphic drawings and effects, such as streamlined shapes and sharp geometrics. Photoshop is programmed in such a way that an image is made up of a mosaic of individual coloured pixels; the software itself does not automatically recognize shapes unless they have been separated out by the user. Motifs that are significantly enlarged, for example, will eventually lose their integrity and become 'pixelated' so that fine lines appear jagged. The total number of pixels over an area is called the resolution, and this determines the quality of the image.

Illustrator creates a graphic image from a series of points, lines, curves and shapes. Sophisticated and high-quality artwork and graphics can be created with the wide range of drawing tools on offer. Once an image is created it can be scaled indefinitely without degradation. It is possible to design solely using either Photoshop or Illustrator, or to work between the two – either way, they offer a perfect toolkit for textile design. The introduction of the digital stylus pen has also given fluidity to the action of drawing with the computer so that it is now more akin to drawing by hand.

Originally designed for the graphics industry, these tools are now leading textile designers along different avenues of creativity and extending the range of design possibilities available to them. Previously, designers were required to hand render their ideas and designs, which was often a time-consuming process, but working within a digital environment has speeded up this task. This allows more time for experimentation and exploration, thus freeing up the designer's imagination. Because these programs are now recognized as standard tools for textile designers, it is essential that you acquire the skills to use them with confidence. Perseverance will lead to being able to use them intuitively, making them just as important as paint and brushes have always been.

This chapter offers inspiration by demonstrating the wealth of possibilities that these programs give to the textile designer. Through a series of step-by-step tutorials focusing on particular techniques that are relevant to textile design, and amply illustrated with work by both students and established designers, this chapter is aimed at students who have already acquired a basic knowledge of Photoshop and Illustrator. It begins by looking at the skills and tools that underlie all good digital textile design, including research and drawing, the use of the scanner, the digital stylus pen and the incorporation of photography.

Jemima Gregson's design, 'New York, New York', was created in Photoshop and digitally printed onto cotton canvas.

Jenny Cooper explored moiré effects in her digital design and print work, 'Interference'. Inspired by contour maps and static interference from television screens, she stretched and manipulated her graphic lines in Illustrator and created soft layers, which she printed digitally onto sheer fabrics such as organza and chiffon to create the moiré effect.

Ross Barnes creates abstract, modernist graphic prints that flood the garment using the gradients in Photoshop. His designs are digitally printed onto a fine silk jersey.

Claire Thorpe's fashion collection, 'Ballet Mécanique', was designed entirely in Illustrator. Her inspiration came from the mechanical patterns found in Meccano toys and also in the work of Eduardo Paolozzi, which she then translated into graphic patterns. Thorpe's designs illustrate the crisp, clean lines that can be achieved using this vector-based program.

GETTING STARTED

When working digitally, the designer is faced with a vast array of options and it is all too easy to get carried away choosing between the technical effects and filters that are available at the click of a button. Consequently, it is vitally important to develop and explore ideas thoroughly before starting to work on the computer.

The starting point for a design can come from one of many sources. It might be a highly personal thought or experience that you want to express visually, or it could come from a commercial brief. Wherever it comes from, thorough research of the subject is essential, and the process can take you on an exciting and stimulating journey; one that may lead you to explore historical periods, other cultures from around the world or contemporary design trends. You may even find inspiration in other creative disciplines such as fine art, literature, science and music. Once a theme is established, the next stage is to gather material to help get the design underway. This can be anything from photographs, sketches and drawings to found objects. It is important not to underestimate the amount of material needed; design work has now become a very sophisticated mix of graphic imagery, drawing, photography, pattern, texture and motif. The more research, the greater the wealth of material you will have to work with, allowing your ideas and concept to develop fully. Explore ideas around the theme and collect anything that relates to it, gathering the material into a sketchbook to track the development of ideas and primary research. This sketchbook can be referenced throughout the design process, and also acts as a basis for discussion with your peers.

At the same time as you are researching your theme, you need to keep the context for your design in mind and research the market. Historically, textile design has always had a very close relationship with fashion, whether for clothing or interiors, and so an awareness of contemporary trends is crucial. In this consumer society, buyers are constantly seeking the next new look. As a textile designer you need market awareness to stay on top of the game in this competitive field.

Louise Townsend scours magazines for relevant fashion influences, and haberdashery stores for fabrics, trimmings and ribbons. This focused research fuels her work. Here, she was developing a theme for a colourful textile collection for the fashion industry, which she exhibited at Indigo, the international textile fair, in Paris in 2006.

Joanna Green built up an inspiration board comprising tearsheets, graphic sketches and colour palettes as a starting point for her textile collection.

Joanna GREEN

Victoria Collins' sketchbook for her collection, 'The Cutting Culture With Character'.

Pages from Rosie MacCurrach's sketchbook for her collection, 'Tales from the Land'.

SCANNING

Once you have gathered together all your material, you then need to assemble it into a form that you can work with digitally. Many of your items will be in two-dimensional form – such as drawings and photographs; others may be three-dimensional – such as buttons, textured fabrics and trimmings. All of these elements can be scanned.

The scanner is an exciting tool for textile designers that has opened up a wide range of options for assembling imagery, allowing non-digital elements into the digital workspace. Designers, who are often magpies by nature, are able to experiment with real objects and imagery that they have collected, collaging them into designs that have a tactile quality and can also be highly personal, humorous, charming and quirky.

Before you start scanning, it is important to know the final print output in dots per inch (dpi), as this determines the resolution required. Ideally, you should scan at the same dpi as the final output, and at the same dimensions as you wish to use the scan in your design. For a textile designer, the final output will usually be a collection of designs that are printed onto fabric or paper – usually A3 to A2 in size. To guarantee a high-quality image at this size, it is best to scan your raw materials at 300 dpi.

If you are outputting the design onto a length of fabric, you need to take more care. Textile designers often work on a large scale and may unwittingly create complex documents with file sizes that are too large to manage. One way to overcome this, if you are working in repeat, is to just give the printer the repeat unit. The printer will then use a specialist repeat program to fill the unit across whatever length of fabric that you require. Giving the repeat unit alone to the printer means that the document size is likely to be manageable, especially as the printer will usually request artwork at between 200 and 300 dpi.

You need to take extra care when working with a large-scale placement or engineered design onto fabric, to maintain a balance between a high-enough resolution and a manageable document size. If you find your final artwork document becomes too large for your computer to manage, you will have to lower the resolution of the image gradually, while assessing the quality of the output.

File sizes generally become large when you scan in objects that are subsequently enlarged by a significant amount. In order to maintain the best photographic quality, scan objects at high resolution, so that when the object is reproduced at 100 percent in your design it is output at the required dpi. The box opposite provides the general rules that will allow you to reproduce good quality imagery for print.

If your artwork is too large for the scanner, you may need to take it to a specialist bureau. A more complicated, but less expensive, alternative is to scan the work in sections and piece it together in Photoshop.

SCANNING QUALITY

FROM A4 TO A1:

Scan your work at 850 dpi;
your A1 artwork will be 300 dpi.

FROM A4 TO A2:

Scan your work at 600 dpi;
your A2 artwork will be 300 dpi.

FROM A4 TO A0:

Scan your work at 1300 dpi;
your A0 artwork will be 300 dpi.

NOTE ON COPYRIGHT

When scanning imagery for use in your designs, it is essential to be aware of copyright issues. Copyright is a form of intellectual property protection. It applies to artists' original work such as paintings, illustration, photographs, maps and any other work of craftsmanship. Scanning opens up a wide range of design opportunities and can sometimes be used as a quick design tool for copying and editing your work, but you must be aware that you should not scan other people's artwork as it may be copyright protected. Either use your own material to avoid infringing on copyright or be sure to use copyright-free imagery.

Kitty Joseph needs time and patience to create her intricate and complex collages from hand-coloured paper. Once she has scanned her collages, however, she uses the speed of the computer to manipulate, compose, colour and edit her artwork further. The ability to preserve her images, once saved, gives her the freedom to experiment with colour and layout without destroying her original artwork.

DRAWING

Drawing, sketching and mark-making have always been solid starting points for design work. They are even more important in the digital age, in ensuring that work is original and that the designer's unique 'handwriting' is not lost, but instead is enhanced, by the computer.

By starting with a beautiful set of drawings, you can scale, compose and arrange them into a design collection using the basic transform tools in Photoshop. There is still skill involved in editing and assembling the drawings and merging them sensitively so that they do not simply look pasted together. Having a thorough understanding of the tools in Photoshop will allow you to choose the best method of selecting a drawing or motif and thereby retaining the feeling of fluid and sensitive artwork. Tools range from the Magic Wand tool (used to select flat colours) to more advanced tools, such as the Mask tool (used to select photography) or the Pen tool (used to draw accurately around an area and cut it out).

Rosie MacCurrach uses the drawings from her sketchbook as a starting point for her digital textile designs. After scanning them in, she meticulously selects areas and builds up compositions in Photoshop. Her aim is to keep the atmospheric qualities of the originals, maintaining the hand-drawn look by blending the drawings together and avoiding a computerized, cut-and-paste look. The quality of her drawings is the basis of her work and the computer becomes just a medium enabling her to assemble them into a design.

To replicate the softness and sensuality of the originals, MacCurrach uses the Quick Mask tool to select her drawings; she also feathers the edges so that the images blend softly together. Finally, she prints her designs onto silk, a fabric that allows her to maintain the delicate marks and blends present in her original drawings.

The computer allows Victoria Purver the freedom to translate her paintings onto fabric without losing any of the beautiful qualities achieved with her brush marks and drawing. She does not have to make colour separations to screen-print them; instead she translates them directly onto fabric through digital printing. Her aim is to keep the sensual feel of the paintings when they are transferred onto cloth.

Helen Kemp scans in her large-scale paintings and prints them digitally onto jersey to use in her menswear collection. Printing digitally allows her to translate her artwork onto fabric without losing the rich brush strokes and hand quality of her work.

Hong Yeon Yun's emotive textile collection, 'How do you feel at 21?', explores the emotional worries of growing up. She interviewed 21-year-olds and then translated thoughts and memories into expressive drawings that capture the strong feelings of being an adolescent. She works freely in mixed media, almost as a painter, and then scans her work at high resolution. Digital printing onto fabric allows her to work with an unlimited colour palette and a wide range of mixed-media techniques.

Brian Barrett's inspiration for his textile collection, 'Classical/contemporary romantic', derives from vintage objects and antiques, including taxidermy. He looks at how collecting objects can harbour memories of the past and create new emotional attachments. Brian created his own take on a traditional floral repeat that, on first viewing, is timeless and familiar. But by subtly weaving unconventional imagery into a traditional layout, the design took on a new meaning and narrative. The result is an intriguing mix of the bizarre and the familiar that creates a new look for textiles by mixing old and new methods in the design and print process.

Zoe Harrington's collection, 'Zoe83', is inspired by the ephemera of childhood. Her designs incorporate imagery relating to the toys and games of the 1980s. She is also influenced by the child-like spirit of work by Eduardo Paolozzi and Jean Michel Basquiat.

Mixing hand-rendered drawings with photography and CAD was the perfect medium for Zoe to express the decade's shift towards digitization. Working in Photoshop allowed her the freedom to spontaneously explore her ideas and digital printing enabled her to translate her photomontage designs directly onto fabric.

THE DIGITAL STYLUS PEN

The introduction of the digital stylus pen has given artists the freedom to draw, paint and sketch with a computer, in much the same way as if using traditional materials. You can draw directly onto a graphics tablet with the pen, or trace over an image, or even draw on the screen. Once mastered, the pen becomes an intuitive drawing tool, allowing the same freedom of movement and sensitivity as a traditional pen or brush. For the textile designer, the pen allows a sensitive and sensual approach to design and is a worthwhile investment. A pressure-sensitive stylus pen can also give depth to your lines, for a more natural way of drawing and rendering. In Photoshop you can even 'harness' the numerous paintbrushes to it, allowing you to create effects ranging from subtle watercolours to bold line drawings. In Illustrator, the pen allows a high degree of dexterity and control when drawing.

Melanie Bowles finds that using the stylus pen gives her the precision she needs to design in Illustrator. Her background in embroidered textiles influences not only her design aesthetic, but also how she uses the computer as a design tool. Melanie finds she can achieve the same dexterity with the stylus pen as with the embroiderer's needle, replicating the intricacies of fine stitch-work found in historical embroideries. Melanie uses the pen to draw streamlined shapes, build up motifs and create subtle blends. She is able to create elegant, graphic designs by directly tracing from found or drawn imagery onto the screen with the pen. When printed onto silks, these designs become fluid and sensual.

PHOTOGRAPHY

Textile designers often make good photographers, having an eye for detail, texture and colour. It is no surprise, therefore, that with the ability to print high-quality photographic detail digitally, many students are now integrating photography into design.

Photography is an immensely useful medium for the textile designer, whether used directly in the design work or as a means of researching and collecting reference material. It can also be useful to draw and trace over photographs in Photoshop or Illustrator as a quick way of achieving an image outline.

The compact size of digital cameras means that many artists and designers use their cameras like sketchbooks or diaries, and are able to build up archives of imagery that they can access when needed. This approach is preferable to downloading images from the Internet because it avoids running into any copyright issues and, of course, the work is unique and personal.

Once you have imported your images into Photoshop you will find a huge number of options to help you adapt your photographs.

Kathryn Round and Charlotte Mann's collection, 'Keep it Country', brings beloved, worn-out garments back to life. The questions they addressed were: 'Why do we discard things we love?' and 'Is there a way we can bring them back to life?' The fashion collection is a photographic remodelling of some of their favourite clothes, all of which have emotional associations. They were digitally printed onto cotton jersey and made into simple, adaptable dresses.

Alexa Ball's womenswear collection, 'Holiday Memories', incorporated childhood holiday photographs into complex pattern formations to achieve a quirky, nostalgic design.

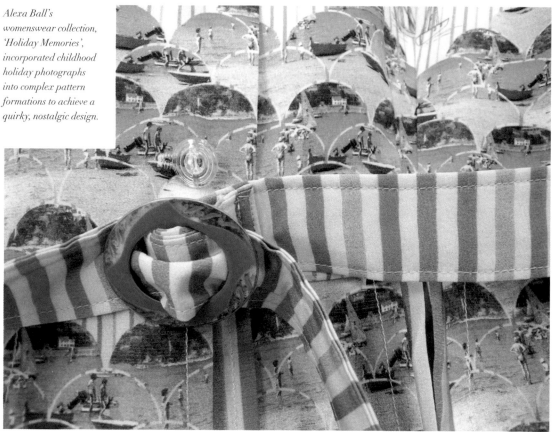

Croatian-born Nada Herceg demonstrates the creative use of photography in her textile collection, 'Kaleidoscope'. Here, she arranged everyday objects and then photographed them through a kaleidoscope, creating these amazing pattern formations. She edited them further by putting them into repeat and printing them digitally onto silk, allowing her to maintain their rich, photographic qualities.

Emma Stone uses a complex process of photography, scanning, drawing and collage techniques to create elaborate and personal textiles.

Working digitally opened up a whole new world for illustrator and designer Emma Stone. It has allowed her to engage with a world of fantasy and surrealism. Her textile collection, 'Recollection', aims to reinvent forgotten pieces and is based on sentimental objects, memories and collections from her family history.

Temitope Tijani plays with caricatures of family members in Photoshop, demonstrating how much fun it can be to integrate photography into design.

Jemima Gregson exploits her love of fashion, photographing treasured pieces and placing them back onto a garment. She enhances her photographs digitally and places them carefully onto specific areas of clothing. The result is witty, glamorous and sexy.

Textile designer Gina Pierce created this piece 'Peeling Paint, Spitalfields', for the Digital Craft on the Fringe exhibition, part of the European Textile Network's 2007 Conference held at London Metropolitan University. The inspiration behind the piece came from the early streets of Spitalfields in east London. Successive influxes of immigrants have left their imprint on the architecture, street names and culture of the area. It is this idea of layered history, often hidden, but sometimes glimpsed, that Pierce wanted to convey. The imagery was taken from the streets of the area, a chair covering, and from early twentieth-century lace.

The image was created in Photoshop and digitally printed onto cotton satin as a piece of fine art. It could, however, also be used for furnishing or printed onto other types of fabric. It shows the photographic quality that is achievable through scanning and digital printing.

TUTORIAL 1
USING FILTERS
IN PHOTOSHOP

There are numerous filters in Photoshop and the choice can seem overwhelming. You will come across new ones all the time while experimenting, and the variety of effects you can create are endless. Be careful not to get carried away with these special effects, though; filters can make your work look obviously 'Photoshopped', as they are very familiar and are often overused. But, if they are carefully integrated as part of the design work, they can add some amazing and subtle effects. Overuse of filters can confuse the design, so be clear from the start about the effect that you want to achieve. You can apply filters to the whole image but they also work well if applied to a selected area of a design. On these pages are just a few examples of filters that are particularly effective for textile design. Use RGB images, as some filters will not work with CMYK.

Daisy Butler's 'Kitsch' furnishing collection is based on Victorian découpage and its love affair with English flowers. She uses a mix of imagery including drawings, photography and Victorian vignettes, which she scans and then composes in Photoshop. She subtly applies filters to areas of her work – in particular the photographs – to give a painted and collaged effect that is reminiscent of a Victorian greetings card.

COLLAGE EFFECTS

Daisy Butler demonstrates the use of the Cutout filter in a subtle way. Here, she selected the roses from her photograph, and applied the Cutout filter. This changed the quality of the photograph to flat, cut-out areas of colour, suitable for the collage effect she wanted to achieve.

DRAWN TEXTURES

There are many rendering effects in the Brush Strokes and Sketch filters in Photoshop. Here, Crosshatch was applied after the Cutout filter was applied, to add a drawn texture.

SIMPLE CUTOUTS

The Cutout filter in Artistic filters lets you turn a photograph into a flat paper cutout. By changing the Levels, Edge Simplicity and Fidelity, you can achieve different grades of simplification.

COLOURED PENCIL

Here, Coloured Pencil filter in Artistic filters was applied to give a bold and vibrant drawn effect. Altering the Pencil Width, Stroke Pressure and Paper Brightness gave an almost 'batik' effect.

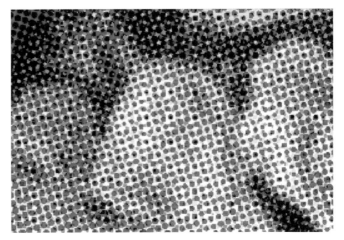

POP ART

The Colour Halftone filter is found in the Pixelate filters, and simulates the effect of using an enlarged halftone screen on each channel of the image. For each channel, the filter divides the image into rectangles and replaces each rectangle with a dot.

This filter will give a photograph a graphic, screen-print effect reminiscent of Pop Art graphics.

3D GRAPHICS

The Extrude filter can be found in the Stylize filters and can give an amazing three-dimensional effect to a design (with either Blocks or Pyramids). It can totally transform the look of an ordinary image into a modern graphic.

EMBROIDERED EFFECTS

The Stained Glass filter is in the Texture filters and will transform a photograph into cells. It can give the effect of embroidery.

ABSTRACT DISTORTIONS

The Wave filter is found in the Distort filters. This will give you, along with the other Distort filters, numerous options with which to abstract and distort a photograph or image into an instant textile design that has fluidity and movement.

RIPPLED EFFECTS

The Glass filter is in the Distort filters and can give an interesting texture to a photograph or design, with a reflective, rippled quality.

SILK-SCREEN EFFECT

Using the Posterize command **(Layer > New Adjustment Layer)** will give a photograph a flat, graphic, but original look, as if you had silk-screened the image.

TUTORIAL 2
CREATING COMPLEX
COLOUR BLENDS

Emamoke Ukeleghe's collection, 'My Family Album', captures the essence of her ethnic background. Her inspiration comes from the journey her family made from Nigeria to England in the mid 1980s. Based on this experience, she has created a collection of digital prints for scarfs and panels that showcases a new contemporary ethnicity.

Ukeleghe replaces the traditional techniques of hand-dyed batik used in African textiles with digital media. Working in Illustrator, she recreates simple geometrics and blends them to give them a rich and exotic feel. Her designs are dynamic, exciting and reminiscent of ethnic textiles, retaining the luminosity of batik printing but with a contemporary twist.

STEP 1

Select the Polygon tool from the Tool palette. Holding down the Shift key, click and drag to create a polygon.

STEP 2

Window > Show Stroke.
Apply a stroke (Weight 2 pt) in a contrasting colour.

STEP 3

Copy and paste the polygon, and change the scale of the copied polygon to 25 percent.
Object > Transform > Scale.
Select both polygons.

STEP 4

Window > Align.
The Align palette will appear.

Vertical Align Centre

Horizontal Align Centre

STEP 5

Select Horizontal Align Centre and Vertical Align Centre to centralize the polygons.

STEP 6

Apply a new Fill and Stroke colour to the central polygon.

STEP 7

Select the Blend tool in the toolbar. Double-click it to reveal the Blend option palette. There are two options: Smooth Blend or Specified Steps. Choose Specified Steps and enter '10'.

STEP 8

Place the Blend tool in the middle of the polygon, drag it to the outer edge and your blend will appear. It's worth experimenting with the options the Blend tool offers to get different effects.

STEP 9

Now create a tile with the polygon. To position it accurately, go to the View menu and select Snap to Point and Smart Guides. Position the pointer on the left-hand anchor point and drag it to the right.

STEP 10

Holding down the Shift and Option/Alt keys, drag the tile across until it snaps into place and leaves a copy. The cursor will turn white when it has snapped to point.

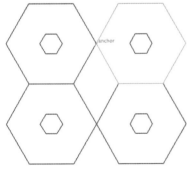

STEP 11

Repeat this action to tile four polygons.

STEP 12

View > Outline.
With the Pen tool, draw a central diamond, clicking on the anchor points as a guide.

STEP 13

Window > Attributes.
A dialogue box will appear. With your diamond selected, select the Show Centre icon. This will show the centre of the diamond.

STEP 14

Make a copy of your diamond, change its scale and place it in the centre of the first diamond.

STEP 15

Fill and Stroke both diamonds with contrast colours.

STEP 16

Now apply a blend to the diamond.

STEP 17

Now open the design unit in Photoshop and put it into a repeat:
Select the design unit.
Edit > Copy.
Create a new Photoshop document at 300 dpi.
Edit > Paste.

STEP 18

A dialogue box will appear. Select the Paste As Pixels option, and click OK.

STEP 19

Another dialogue box will appear. Click Place.

STEP 20

View > Show Rulers.
View > Show Guides.

STEP 23

Select > Select All.

STEP 21

Bring down horizontal and vertical guides to the centre points of all four polygons.

STEP 22

Select the Crop tool from the Tool palette and, using the guides, crop the unit.

STEP 24

Edit > Define Pattern.

STEP 25

Create a new document.
Edit > Fill > Pattern.

TUTORIAL 3
BUILDING FLORAL MOTIFS

'Making Flowers' is a collection of digital prints created by Melanie Bowles. With Illustrator she creates clean, graphic florals that give her work a striking, contemporary look.

This tutorial shows you the principles of creating flowers in Illustrator by making a basic petal, and then duplicating and rotating it to build up a complex flower. You can build up ornate patterns from the basic design. The possibilities are endless for the textile designer who wishes create a fresh, bold floral look.

STEP 1

First, create the basic petal shapes.
Reveal a grid on your document
page to help you create them.
View > Show Grid.
Work in the Outline mode to create petals.
View > Outline.
Now use the Pen tool to create
your basic petal shapes.

STEP 2

View > Preview.
Fill your shapes with black.
Select one petal.
Edit > Copy.

STEP 3

Open up a new document, and again
reveal the grid.
Edit > Paste.

Rotate tool

STEP 4

Now build the flower up.
Window > Info.
With the petal selected, select the Rotate
tool from the Tool palette, and place it at
the bottom of the petal.
Hold down the Option/Alt key and rotate
the petal (this will make a copy of your
petal as you rotate it).

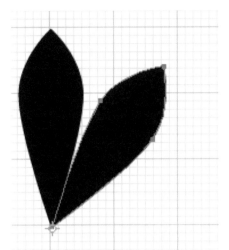

STEP 5

To enter an accurate angle for your petal to rotate, with the Rotate tool still selected, place the reference point at the bottom of the petal. Now press Option/Alt and click, and the Rotate menu will appear. Enter an angle that is a division of 360 degrees. Click on the Copy button, and a second petal will appear.

STEP 6

Once you have placed the second petal correctly, you can build up the other petals to complete the flower.
Press Control/Command + D;
this keyboard shortcut will repeat the last command.
Once you have a complete flower, group the petals together.
Object > Group.

STEP 7

Now apply a colour fill. Copy and paste several times to build the flower up, changing the scale and colour of each copy.

STEP 8

Window > Align.

Align Vertically   Align Horizontally

STEP 9

With the Rotate tool, rotate the flowers. Alter the transparency of the petals to give an impression of depth.
Finally, group the completed flower.
Object > Group.

STEP 10

Draw a line and a circle for the stamen.
Object > Group.
Now copy and rotate the stamen, using the same method as for the petals.

STEP 11

The flower is complete.
Object > Group.

STEP 12

Create more flowers using the same techniques, selecting different colours and sizes of petals.

TUTORIAL 4
CROSS-STITCH EFFECTS

Claire Thorpe devised this effective technique in Illustrator to fill motifs with cross-stitch without even touching a needle.

This tutorial demonstrates how to create a cross-stitch pansy, but you could also apply the same technique using another stitch or simple motif.

STEP 1

Select the Line tool from the Tool palette. Draw a 45-degree line by holding down the Shift key at the same time as clicking and dragging.

STEP 2

Go to the option bar at the top of the screen. Click on the Link icon between the width and the height. Enter '0.2 cm'.

STEP 3

Go to the Stroke palette and enter the Weight: '2 pt'.
Select Round Edge.

STEP 4

Select the cross. Double-click on the Reflect tool in the Tool palette.
Select Vertical, 90 degrees and Copy.
Select Both Lines and **Object > Group**.

STEP 5

Press the Return key to bring up the Move dialogue box. Enter '-0.27 cm' in the Vertical field. This is the measurement from the centre of the cross to the centre of the repeated cross. (In this case it is -0.27 cm. If your cross is bigger, the measurement to your repeated cross will be larger, depending on the gap you want between them.)
Click on Copy, and the second cross will appear. Press Control/Command + D repeatedly to build up a vertical line of crosses.

STEP 6

Select the vertical line of crosses.
Press the Return key to bring up the
Move dialogue box. Enter '0.27 cm' in the
Horizontal field and click on Copy.
Press Control/Command + D repeatedly to
build up horizontal rows of crosses.
Your cross-stitch grid is now complete.

STEP 7

Create a new layer and place it underneath
your stitch grid.
File > Place.
Find the motif that you wish to place.
Go back to the stitch grid layer.
Edit > Select All.
Colour the stroke grey.
Lower the Transparency to reveal the
motif template.

STEP 8

Now carefully colour each individual stitch
to build up the motif.

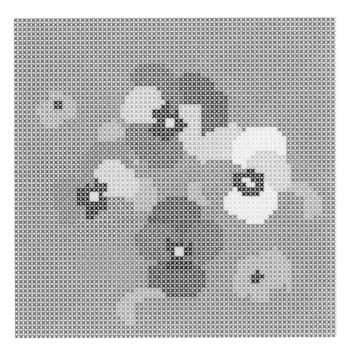

STEP 9

Select one of the grid stitches.
Select > Same > Stroke Weight.
All the stitches of that colour will be
selected. With this method you can
re-colour your design or delete the stitches
and just keep the stitched motif.

TUTORIAL 5
ENGINEERED PRINTS

'Jemima's World' is an inspirational fashion collection by Jemima Gregson, based on her love of vintage costume jewellery. Jemima places photographs of her jewellery onto the garment shapes in Photoshop to create a stunning trompe l'œil effect, which also shows the exceptional photographic qualities that can be achieved with digital printing. The garment shapes are digitally printed onto silk satin using a Mimaki TX2, and then made into a garment.

This tutorial demonstrates the process of engineering a print onto a garment shape using Photoshop.

STEP 1

Scan in your pattern pieces at 300 dpi, starting with the front. You will have to do this in several sections. Once they are scanned in, paste the sections together.

STEP 2

Reposition the top front section of the garment on the canvas by moving it to the top.

STEP 3

Edit > Canvas Size.
A dialogue box with the central square highlighted will appear. Alter the Width and Height measurements sufficiently to allow you to paste in the bottom section of the garment.
Once this is done, flatten the image.

STEP 4

Now increase the canvas size to fit the complete garment shape.
Edit > Canvas Size.
Change the Width to 200 percent.
Click OK.

STEP 5

Select the garment piece with the Marquee tool.
Copy and Paste.
Edit > Transform > Flip Horizontally.
Piece the two shapes together so that they match up.
Flatten the image.

Fill option

STEP 6

Select the Pen tool, and the option bar will appear. Select the Fill option with black as the foreground colour in the toolbar.

STEP 7

Carefully trace around the garment using the Pen tool, to create a series of anchor points around the garment shape. Use the Convert Point tool (in the Pen tool menu) to create the curves around the neck and armholes. It may take some time and practice until you are happy with the results.

STEP 8

When you use the Pen tool, a shape layer will appear in the Layers palette. Change the Opacity of this layer to reveal the pattern shape so you can trace over it.

STEP 9

Continue to draw around the garment shape with the Pen tool until it is complete. When you use the Pen tool, you create a new path. Go to the Path palette to see your new path. Click on the arrow on the right to reveal the drop-down menu. Save your new path so you can edit or select it at any time.

STEP 10

Repeat the entire process with the back sections of the garment.

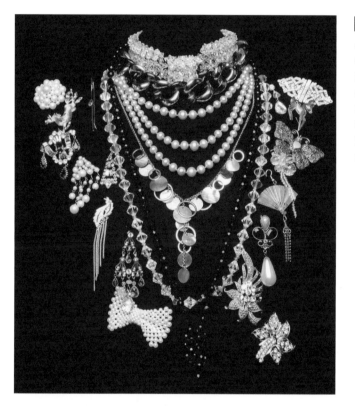

STEP 11

Arrange a selection of costume jewellery onto a mannequin covered in black material. Using a digital SLR camera and studio lighting, photograph the mannequin at the highest possible resolution. This will allow the image to be reproduced at the maximum size with no compromise in quality.

STEP 12

You could also photograph some extra jewellery against a black background to add to the mannequin jewellery.

STEP 13

Open up the front garment shape. Your path is drawn but you need to make it into a selection so you can start to paste your jewellery into the pattern piece.

STEP 14

On the Path palette, highlight your path and click the Path Selection icon at the bottom of the palette. This will create a selection for you to paste your jewellery into.

Path Selection icon

STEP 15

Open up the mannequin photograph. You may wish to brighten the jewellery.
Image > Adjustments > Brightness/Contrast.
Alter the sliders to adjust the tonal range until you are happy with the effect.
Select > All.
Edit > Copy.

STEP 16

Now open up the front garment image. Select the garment shape.
Go > Edit > Paste Into.
With the new pasted-in layer selected, click the Move tool and position your jewellery to fit into the garment shape. Scale it to fit.
Edit > Transform > Scale.

STEP 17

Merge the shape layer and the jewellery layer using the Merge Visible command in the Layer palette.

STEP 18

With the Clone tool, carefully clone the necklace to make it continue around the neckline.

STEP 19

Open the extra photographs, and select items with the Lasso tool. **Edit > Copy**.

STEP 20

Now go back to the garment shape and paste on new jewellery.
Edit > Paste.
Merge the new layers as you go. Lower the Transparency of the jewellery layer so that it reveals the pattern piece beneath.
Continue to add more images to build up the design.

STEP 21

Once you have completed the front, use the same techniques to complete the back and cuffs. When they are all finished, flatten the layers.
Now open a document with a Width of 140 cm (55 in) – the width of fabric on the digital printer – and a Height of 150 cm (59 in). Set the Resolution to 200 dpi. Open each garment piece.
Select > All > Copy.
Go to your new fabric length document and paste the garment piece on.
Edit > Paste.
Paste all the garment shapes and arrange them across the final document.

STEP 22

Once the shapes are placed, flatten the layers. Now you are ready to prepare the document for printing.

TUTORIAL 6
SEQUIN EFFECTS

'You can't hurry love' is a fashion collection created by Tennessee-born Katie Irving Jones. The collection is intended to elicit a sentimental attachment, and draws inspiration from nostalgic heirlooms that Katie incorporates into her designs. She recreates vintage embellishments using digital techniques in Photoshop.

This tutorial demonstrates how to create a sequin motif. Once the technique is mastered, it can be applied to any design.

STEP 1

Scan a sequin at 300 dpi.
**Select > Image >
Adjustments > Levels**.
Adjust the shadow and highlights by
moving the sliders in the dialogue box.

STEP 2

Add a lens flare on the corner of the
sequin to give it an extra twinkle.
Filter > Render > Lens Flare.

STEP 3

Select the sequin with the Magic Wand
tool. Set the Tolerance in the option bar to
30 and select an area around the sequin.
Edit > Cut. Cut away the background.
Select the sequin with the Marquee tool.
Edit > Define Brush. Name the sequin.

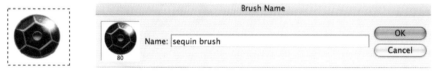

STEP 4

Make a drawing of a heart and banner and
scan it into Photoshop. Create a new layer.
Select the new sequin brush.
In the Brush Option palette, change the
Opacity to 93 percent and the Size to
70 pixels.

STEP 5

Select black as the brush colour and
'stamp' around the outline of the heart
in black sequins, by clicking once to
apply each.

STEP 6

Now add a slight shadow to this layer
to give it a three-dimensional effect.
Go to the Layer Style icon at the bottom
of the Layer palette.

Layer Style icon

STEP 7

In the Layer Style palette, select Drop Shadow. A drop-down menu will appear. Change the Opacity and the Distance values to create a soft shadow.

STEP 8

Create a new layer.
Select the sequin brush and choose a dark red colour.
Stamp inside the heart as shown.

STEP 9

Create a new layer.
Fill the rest of the heart with the sequin brush coloured bright red.
You should now have four layers.
Turn the Background layer off and merge the visible layers.

Line tool option bar

STEP 10

Next, create the stitches that appear to fasten each sequin to give the hand-sewn effect. This is a fairly time-consuming process, but is still a lot quicker than actually sewing them!
Select the Line tool from the Tool palette. Make sure the Fill option is selected in the option bar.

STEP 11

The Line tool option bar will appear at the top of your screen. For Weight, type '3 px' and select a colour for the stitch. Now draw in every stitch, working on each separate layer. Make them slightly irregular to achieve a truly hand-sewn effect. Your sequins are now complete. Fill in the background layer with white and flatten the image.

STEP 12

Next you need to create the 'LOVE' lettering. Scan the lettering into Photoshop.

STEP 13

Use the same technique as before to stamp around the lettering with the sequin brush, varying the scale of the brush.

STEP 14

Once the lettering is complete, flatten the layers and cut it out with the Marquee tool.
Edit > Copy.
Open the heart motif.
Edit > Paste.
Position and adjust the lettering with the Transform tools to fit inside the banner.

STEP 15

Finally, add an extra glow to the finished heart motif.
Filter > Render > Lens Glare.

STEP 16

Print the design onto opaque transfer T-shirt paper through a desktop inkjet printer. Carefully cut the motif out and press it onto your fabric with an iron or heat-press.

TUTORIAL 7
PHOTOMONTAGE

Photomontage is the technique of combining photographic elements together to create new compositions. The introduction of Photoshop has made achieving a photomontage effect faster and easier. There is now a trend towards combining illustration, graphics and photography to create complex designs.

Creating photomontage in Photoshop depends on developing a theme and having a collection of visually strong photographs to work with. Once you have these, you need to select elements from them and start to build new configurations. You will need to work with the more advanced selection tools to achieve the best edge quality. The most effective tool for selecting areas of photographs is the Mask tool. By using the Airbrush to make selections, you can also achieve soft edges; this tool is easiest to control with a stylus pen.

STEP 1

Open up your source image (make sure it is in RGB, as you will apply a filter later). Click on the Mask tool located at the bottom of the Tool palette.

→ Mask tool

STEP 2

Choose a soft airbrush (using the Brush option) and paint over the image you want to mask. This will appear transparent red. Don't worry if you go over the edges.

STEP 3

Switch the foreground colour to white to use the Mask Eraser tool. Select a small, soft brush and start to clean up the edges of the mask.

STEP 4

To exit the Quick Mask mode, click on the Standard Mode icon. The area outside of the mask will now be selected.

STEP 5

Now select the Pansy.
Select > Inverse.

Standard Mode icon

STEP 6

Open a new document.
File > Copy.
File > Paste.

Continue to build a posey from the photographs you have, using the same Quick Mask process to select a flower from your photograph. Copy and paste the flowers and arrange them into a posey with the Move tool.

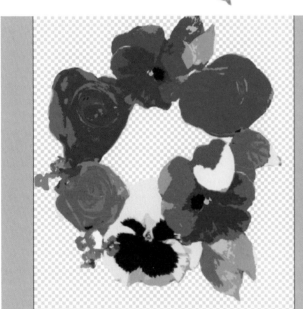

STEP 8

Turn the background layer off and merge the visible layers.

STEP 9

To achieve a collage effect, apply the Cutout Filter.
Filter > Artist > Cutout
Experiment wit the levels until you are happy with the result.

STEP 10

Open a new document, 1 x 1 cm (³/₈ x ³/₈ in) and create a spot.

STEP 11

Define > Pattern.

STEP 12

Select the background layer.
Edit > Fill > Pattern. Find your spot.

STEP 13

Finally, scan in another image and copy and paste it into the centre of the design.

Good photography and careful selection of areas is
the basis of creating successful photomontage designs.
This group of photographs by Daisy Butler formed the
basic elements of her design. The photographs are all
300 dpi to maintain a high-resolution image.

TUTORIAL 8

BUILDING A
BRUSH PALETTE

The Brushes palette is one of the most versatile tools for textile design in Photoshop. It allows you to create your own custom brush from almost any mark or motif, and then paint freely with it. Designs can be created instantly using your custom brush, or the brush may just be a useful tool to add your own elements to a design.

The inspiration behind this whimsical textile collection, by Korean-born Hong Yeon Yun, came from childhood memories of her garden. Her designs are mainly produced using brushes created in Photoshop from her drawings.

The Brushes palette in Photoshop affords the same fluidity and spontaneity that painting does. This, combined with her quirky drawings, adds a magical element to her work. The design shown here is made up from 23 brushes produced in Photoshop; by layering the brushes and changing their scale, rotation and scattering, Hong Yeon Yun has created a rich and complex collection of designs that maintain the lyrical feeling of her drawings.

This tutorial demonstrates how to use brushes and also shows how to create a basic half-drop with the design.

STEP 1

First, create the series of brushes that you will use to produce your design. You may choose a motif for each brush from a shape you have drawn in Illustrator or from a drawing scanned into Photoshop. Either way, it is best if the initial motif is black to allow maximum definition when you come to customize it. If you are following the tutorial exactly, you may wish to scan in the motifs shown here.

STEP 2

Use the Magic Wand tool to select a motif. (In this case, the butterfly.)

STEP 3

Edit > Define Brush Preset.
Name your brush.
Your new brush will be saved in the Brushes palette. Create a whole series of brushes in the same way.

STEP 4

Open the Brushes palette.
Windows > Brushes.
Within this palette you have endless choices for editing your brushes. Do this by adjusting the various sliders; it is worth experimenting with these options to see the effects that can be achieved.

STEP 5

Open a new document and a new layer. With the tree-trunk brush (or one of your own brushes), choose a colour and size and paint a tree trunk by clicking once.

Open another new layer. This will give you the chance to try a few effects, deleting and remaking layers until you are satisfied.

Choose the leaf brush from the Brushes palette and select Shape Dynamics. Change the Size Jitter and Angle Jitter parameters.

Select the Scattering option. Adjust the Scatter, Count and Count Jitter.

Size Jitter

Shape Dynamics

Angle Jitter

Select Colour Dynamics. Select a foreground and background colour in the Tool palette. Adjust the sliders in the Colour Dynamics dialogue box.

Finally, determine the Opacity by clicking on Other Dynamics and moving the Opacity slider. Your leaf brush is ready; start scattering the leaves.

Foreground colour

Background colour

Continue to scatter the leaves until the tree is complete.
Fill the background layer with a colour.

Create a new layer and select the flower stem brush. Select the Shape Dynamics option and slightly change the Angle Jitter. Paint the flower stems, changing the scale as you go if you wish.

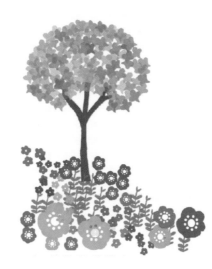

STEP 11

Create a new layer for the flowers. Again, change the foreground and background colours to change the colour effects in the Colour Dynamics option.

STEP 12

Build up the flowers to surround the tree.

STEP 13

Create a new layer and scatter some hearts around the tree.

STEP 14

Now that your design is nearly complete you will have several layers. Turn the background layer off and flatten the visible layers. You should now have two layers: the background layer and the design layer. Save a copy of the image with a new name.

STEP 15

Create another new layer and place it under the design layer. Add other motifs to fill in the spaces. Do not let any of the motifs go over the edges of the design.

STEP 16

Now go to the background layer and change the colour if you wish.
Finally, flatten the image.
Layer > Flatten Image.

STEP 17

The next stage is to put the design into a simple half-drop repeat.
Select > All.
Edit > Copy.

STEP 18

Go to **Filter > Other > Offset**.
Move the Vertical slider to cut the image in half. (Ensure Wrap Around is selected.)

Offset

| Horizontal: | +10 | pixels right | OK |
| Vertical: | +808 | pixels down | Cancel |

☑ Preview

Undefined Areas
○ Set to Transparent
○ Repeat Edge Pixels
● Wrap Around

STEP 19

Go to the Tool palette and make sure the background colour is the same as your design background colour.

→ Background colour

STEP 20

Image > Canvas size.
Highlight the middle box on the left-hand side.
Change the Width to 200 percent.

Canvas Size

Current Size: 5.29M
Width: 99.06 mm
Height: 133.86 mm

OK
Cancel

Current document height

New Size: 10.6M
Width: 200 | percent
Height: 100 | percent
☐ Relative
Anchor:

Canvas extension color: Background

STEP 21

View > Snap to > All.

STEP 22

Edit > Paste.
Snap your design into position. Flatten the layers.

STEP 23

Your half-drop repeat is now complete.
If you wish to change the unit size go to
Image > Image Size.

STEP 24

Select > All.
Edit > Define Pattern.
Name your pattern.

TUTORIAL 9
TEXTURED EFFECTS

Claire Turner's collection is a quirky mixture of screen-printed fabrics and digital prints. She combines digital photography with her lovely freehand drawings. Her grass-printed dress (below right) demonstrates how to create an all-over texture print, and also shows how effective a photographic print can be. This technique can also be useful to create a background onto which you can apply images or motifs.

STEP 1

Start with a photograph approximately 20 x 20 cm (8 x 8 in) at 300 dpi. You will put it into a continuous repeat so there are no obvious seam lines.

STEP 2

Image > Size.
Jot down the pixel size of your image.

STEP 3

Filter > Other > Offset.

STEP 4

Divide the Horizontal and the Vertical pixel image sizes by two and enter the new values.

Seam

STEP 5

Your image will be cut into four and flipped round so the outside of the image is in repeat. You will see a seam appear.

STEP 6

The best tool for mending a photographic texture is the Clone tool. This will copy one area into another. In the Clone tool option bar you can choose different brushes and change the Opacity. By using an airbrush you will get a softer effect.

STEP 7

Select the Clone tool. Choose an area of the design that you want to clone, and press the Alt/Option key to set the copy target point. Move the Clone tool onto the seam and start mending it (see mended section on left-hand side of this image). Keep resetting the target copy point and mending until you achieve a seamless join. This process can take some time.

STEP 8

Once the mending is complete, you can put your unit into repeat. At this point you can change its size if you wish.
Edit > Image > Size. Choose percent and alter as required.

STEP 9

Select > All.

STEP 10

Edit > Define Pattern.

STEP 11

Open a new document.
Edit > Fill > Pattern. Find your pattern. Check your pattern repeat for obvious seams or lines. If you see any you can go back to the original unit and amend, then remake the pattern until you are satisfied.

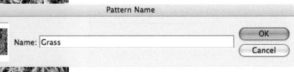

Pattern Name

Name: Grass

OK

Cancel

CREATING A GOOD REPEAT

When putting a textural design into repeat, the aim is to create a continuous pattern. There should be no clumsy interruptions that stand out and make a design look awkward. After a few attempts it should be perfectly possible to create repeats where the repetition of the unit is not apparent unless the viewer really searches for it. Rhythm and balance are the key to a good repeat.

The photograph on the right was the starting point for this example. The largest possible area, containing only the shells, was cropped and put into a half-drop repeat (see page 96). A half-drop is the best method for disguising the joins of textural repeat. In this process the seams are blended using the Clone tool.

The best method for checking your repeat is successful is to reduce the file size and tile-out as large an area as possible (at least two units across and down), then stand back and see if any unintentional patterns emerge.

BAD REPEAT

This example is not as successfully crafted as it could be. This is because certain elements, such as the emptier patches of sand and the diagonal line of larger white shells, stand out too obviously. One way of avoiding this is to scatter any eye-catching elements so they do not line up and so that the eye moves around the design rather than focusing on an isolated element.

GOOD REPEAT

In this example of a successful repeat, some of these same shells were carefully selected, copied and repositioned around the unit and finally blended into the background so that they were more evenly distributed. Some were also rotated so they look like slightly different motifs.

TUTORIAL 10
CREATING A
COLOUR PALETTE

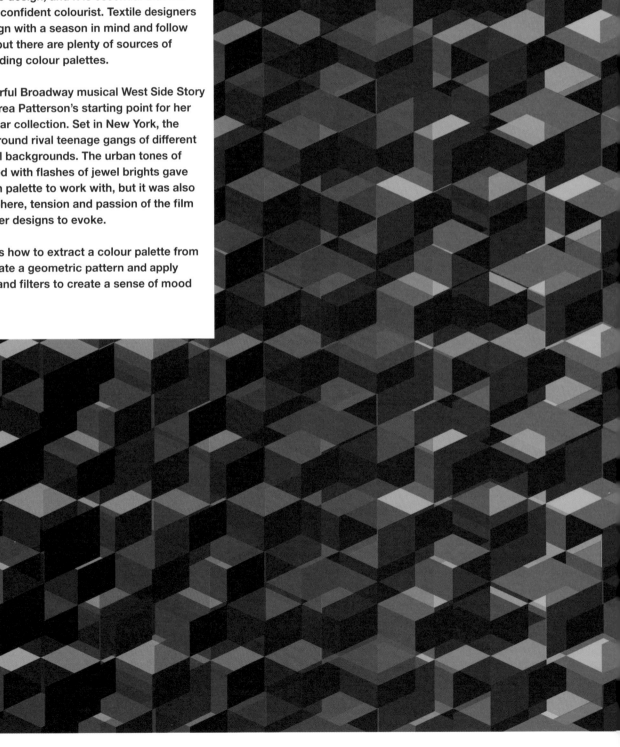

Colour is one of the most important elements in creating a successful textile design, and it is essential that the designer can be a confident colourist. Textile designers often have to design with a season in mind and follow colour forecasts, but there are plenty of sources of inspiration for building colour palettes.

A film of the powerful Broadway musical West Side Story was designer Andrea Patterson's starting point for her winter womenswear collection. Set in New York, the musical centres around rival teenage gangs of different ethnic and cultural backgrounds. The urban tones of gritty city life mixed with flashes of jewel brights gave the designer a rich palette to work with, but it was also the mood, atmosphere, tension and passion of the film that she wanted her designs to evoke.

This tutorial shows how to extract a colour palette from a photograph, create a geometric pattern and apply colouring effects and filters to create a sense of mood and atmosphere.

STEP 1

Open up your photograph in Illustrator.
Select All
Filter > Create > Object Mosaic.

STEP 2

A drop-down menu will appear, choose how many tiles you want vertically and horizontally.
In this example 25 have been selected. The Tiles will be grouped – to ungroup them go to **Object > Ungroup**.

STEP 3

Select a random series of tiles from the mosaic that represent a colour grouping you like.
Copy > Paste.
Select individual tiles and, with the Eyedropper tool, move across the mosaic and select and drop colours to create a palette. Alternatively, you could use a combination already together in the mosaic.

STEP 4

Here the designer has created two separate palettes from the mosaic that capture the mood she wants to evoke. To create a new palette, open up the Swatch palette if it is not already visible **Window > Swatches**.
Delete colours from the Swatch palette. Now highlight the individual tiles from your selected colours and click on the New Swatch icon at the bottom of the palette to create new swatches.

New Swatch icon

STEP 5

Click on the right-hand arrow in the Swatch box to reveal the drop-down menu. Scroll down to Save Swatch Library. Name your new swatch palette. This will now be saved and you can access it at any time from the Swatch Library.

STEP 6

Open Swatch palette and find your saved colour palette in the Swatch Library.

New Swatch...
Duplicate Swatch
Merge Swatches
Delete Swatch

Spot Colors...

Select All Unused

Sort by Name
Sort by Kind
Show Find Field

✓ Small Thumbnail View
Large Thumbnail View
List View

Swatch Options...

Open Swatch Library ▶
Save Swatch Library...
Save Swatches for Exchange...

Save Palette as Swatch Library

Save As: West side story.ai

Where: Swatches

Use Adobe Dialog

Cancel   Save

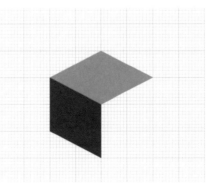

STEP 7

Open up a new document.
View > Show Grid
View > Snap to Grid
View > Smart Guides on.
With the grid as a guide, begin to draw a cube. Your points will snap to the grid.

STEP 8

Once your cube is complete, select the whole cube, **Object > Group. View > Undo Snap to Grid Snap to Point.**

STEP 9

Select the cube, with the Select tool placed directly on the far left anchor point. Hold down the Shift key and the Option/Alt key and drag and copy the first cube until it snaps into place on the right-hand anchor point of the cube and leaves a copy. When the double arrow goes white it has snapped to point.

STEP 10

Press Command + D to repeat the last command and duplicate your cube. Build up a row.

STEP 11

Once you have a row **Object > Ungroup** the cube so you can colour individual sides with your colour palette. When your row is coloured, **Select > All Object > Group**.

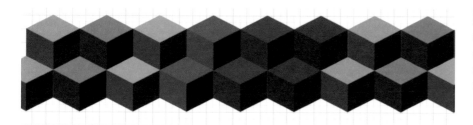

STEP 12

Select the row and, holding down the Shift and Alt keys as before, duplicate the entire row this time. Continue until you have built up a unit of cubes.

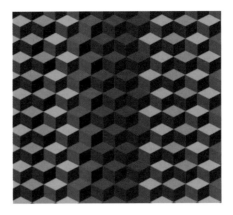

STEP 13

To tidy up the edges, draw a rectangle
(with no Stroke or Fill) over the design,
and use the Crop tool to neaten the edge.
With the rectangle selected,
Select > All.

STEP 14

Object > Clipping Mask > Make.
Save your design. Export the design
as a tiff file
File > Export.

ADDING FILTERS AND EFFECTS

**There are many effects and filters that can be used in
Photoshop but Andrea wanted to maintain the colour and
energy that initially inspired her in the musical. Her aim is to
give the design a sense of movement and rhythm that the
dance scene evokes.**

TRANSPARENT OVERLAYS
STEP 1

Open the design in Photoshop and
duplicate the layer twice.
Select the second layer, **Edit > Transform
> Scale** and enlarge the layer. Alter the
opacity in the Layer palette to reveal the
underneath layer, and with the Move tool
slightly shift the layer across to reveal
the layer beneath.

STEP 2

With this layer still selected go to Blend
Modes, which are at the top of the Layer
palette, to reveal the blend options.
On Layer three, apply the Hue blend to
heighten the colour. Experiment with the
opacity in the Layer palette to enhance the
effects of transparency and movement.

MAKING WAVES

Flatten all the layers.
Filter > Distort > Wave.
Alter the sliders in the Wave palette until you are happy with the effect.

COLOUR BLENDS

Here, a different colour palette has been used to create the cubes. After exporting your design to Photoshop, again duplicate the layers, changing the scale and opacity in the Layer palette, and add the Blend Modes settings Difference and Lighten to create the effect shown on the left.

Finally, flatten the image and apply the Liquifying Filter in the Filter Options to create fluidity and colour blending.

CHAPTER 3
PATTERNS
AND REPEATS

PATTERNS AND REPEATS IN DIGITAL TEXTILE DESIGN

Artists and designers have always been inspired by both the natural and man-made textures and patterns that surround them, and repeating patterns have formed the basis of most surface design in the decorative arts. It seems that we are instinctively drawn to designs that mimic the rhythms found in nature.

If a design is hand painted or drawn then the pattern may be made to change continuously, in the same way that ripples in water vary, and yet also seem to follow a predictable structure. In traditional mechanized printing, however, this kind of randomization is not possible and the exact repetition of motifs is an intrinsic part of the process. The introduction of digital printing means that such rigid repetition is no longer necessary. But there are still sound aesthetic and practical reasons for putting a design into repeat.

There are two types of repeat structure used to lay out a design, so that once printed it will form a continuous length: the block or tile, and the half-drop repeat. It may not seem obvious at first, but all surface designs that have been printed by traditional mechanical methods fit into one of these two structures. Examples of tiled repeats include chequerboards, plaids and stripes, while half-drops include polka dots, diamonds and ogees, as well as the familiar pattern in which bricks are often laid.

An obvious and intentional geometric structure is part of the very nature of a plaid or diamond design. In the case of more organic patterns, such as floral or textural designs, where the designer does not intend to lay out the motifs geometrically, a successful repeat is one that is not obvious, but instead creates an illusion of randomly scattered motifs or unbroken texture (see page 79). Such textural designs tend to be more meditative and restful to the eye, in contrast to patterns in which the repeat structure is intended to dominate the design, making a bold statement. Both styles can be equally pleasing.

A skilled repeat artist is able to put an organic design based on pebbles or woodgrain together in such a way that a viewer who is not searching for the repeat unit will not be aware of it. In an example of a repeat that has not been well constructed, a particularly bright pebble might perhaps stand out from the rest as it was repeated, drawing the viewer's eye to this one element and destroying the illusion of a natural surface.

This problem, known as 'tracking' within the surface design industry, where an unintentional stripe or diagonal has been created, can be resolved by scattering copies or variations of noticeable elements in a design in such a way that they appear to be randomly placed and equally balanced with other similar motifs or coloured areas. An important factor in carrying out this randomization is to make sure that the initial size of the repeat unit is large enough to contain enough elements with which to work. This may be accomplished by joining several images together to form the unit that will then be repeated. All of us have seen this type of repeat in the textures often used in kitchen Formica or linoleum, based on photographs of marble, for example. In the case of a floral, a balanced rhythm can be created by rotating and mirroring motifs until the overall effect is fluid and the eye is not distracted by a rigid structure. A balanced distribution of negative space is also crucial.

By using digital techniques and 'stepping out' – or tiling – your design in repeat on-screen, prior to printing, you have the option of rectifying any visual mistakes such as tracking. If tracking does occur, then you should rework and re-tile the repeat until you achieve a balanced effect.

CREATING REPEATS IN PHOTOSHOP AND ILLUSTRATOR

Putting your design into repeat is the final stage of preparing your work for production. It is vital that you understand repeat structures and how they can change the look of a design, and the different approaches that can be explored. Prior to the introduction of software such as Photoshop, repeats were created by tracing or photocopying the original artwork, cutting up the page and collaging or retracing motifs to work across the seam. Once the repeat unit was deemed successful, the design would be recreated by painting or photocopying. The methods explained in this chapter for creating a repeat digitally follow the same principles, though are obviously far less time-consuming.

Even though Photoshop and Illustrator were not created for textile designers, there are many methods for creating repeats using these programs. Photoshop offers a painterly approach to design work; for example, the Clone tool may be used to maintain the hand-drawn or photographic qualities of an original design. The tools can help when mending any of the seams that are inevitably created during the repeat process, which must be done with skill.

Illustrator, on the other hand, is a vector-based program and the software maintains a mathematical 'memory' of elements so that they never become distorted during manipulation. It is easier to set up groups of motifs in Illustrator than in Photoshop so that they may all be moved or manipulated together. Accurate and complex graphic patterns and constructions can be built in this program, providing an infinite range of possibilities.

This chapter presents tutorials designed to explain the basic principles of setting up block and half-drop repeats in both

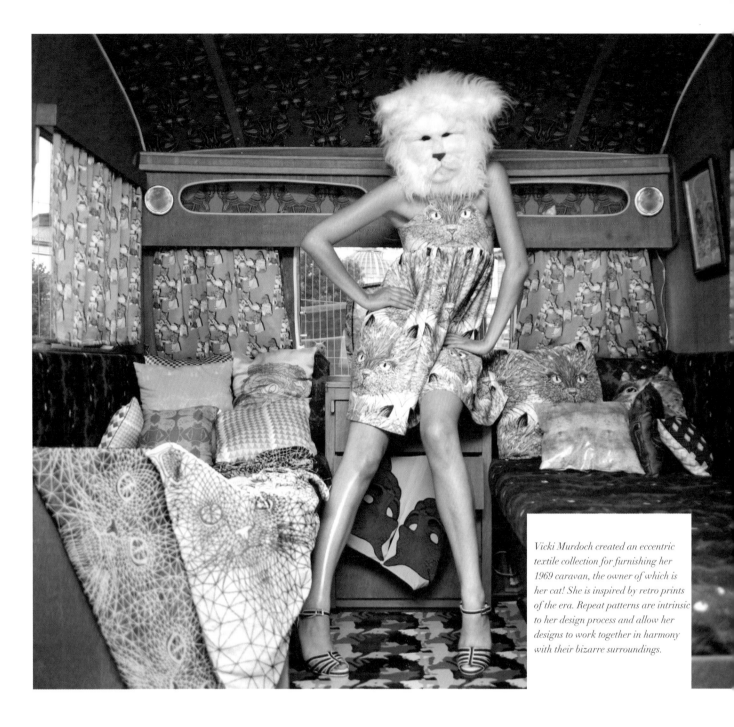

Vicki Murdoch created an eccentric textile collection for furnishing her 1969 caravan, the owner of which is her cat! She is inspired by retro prints of the era. Repeat patterns are intrinsic to her design process and allow her designs to work together in harmony with their bizarre surroundings.

Photoshop and Illustrator; examples include stripes and plaids. Once you have mastered the mechanical processes in both programs they should become second nature, allowing you to concentrate on designing and constructing successful repeats. Photoshop is better suited to organic, painterly or photographic designs, while Illustrator works well with geometric and hard-edged styles.

Specialist textile design software geared for production and the preparation of designs for traditional print production, such as AVA, Pointcarré and Lectra, does exist and will be covered more fully in Chapter Six. Many of these systems have the advantage of providing more sophisticated functions for creating repeats that are considerably faster than off-the-shelf packages such as Photoshop and Illustrator.

TUTORIAL 11

PHOTOSHOP REPEAT
BASIC BLOCK
REPEAT

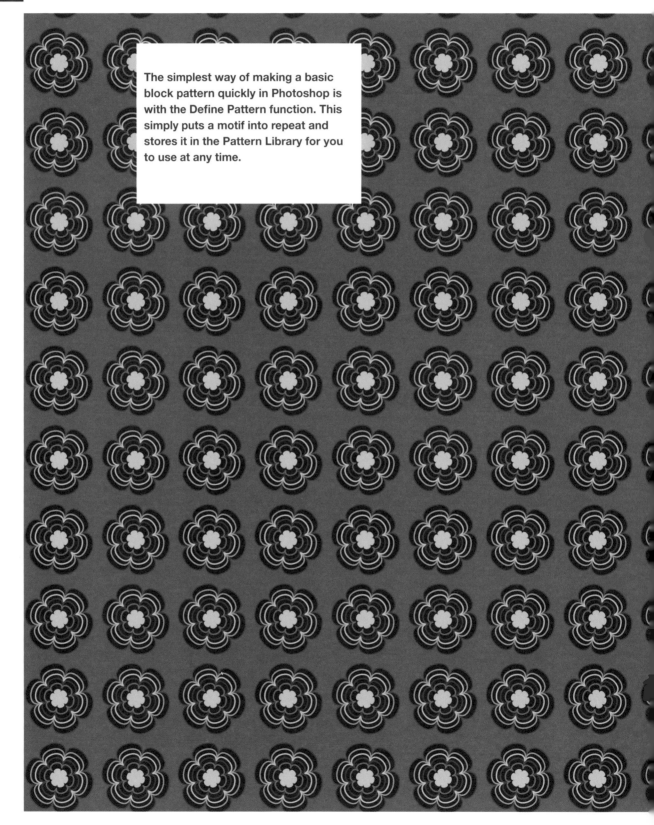

The simplest way of making a basic block pattern quickly in Photoshop is with the Define Pattern function. This simply puts a motif into repeat and stores it in the Pattern Library for you to use at any time.

STEP 1

Choose a motif and resize the unit to the required size. Here the image was scaled to 2 x 2 cm ($^4/_5$ x $^4/_5$ in).
Edit > Image Size.
Select > All.

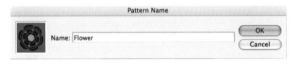

STEP 2

Edit > Define Pattern.
Name your new pattern.

Edit	Image	Layer	Select	Filte
Undo Crop				⌘Z
Step Forward				⇧⌘Z
Step Backward				⌥⌘Z
Fade...				⇧⌘F
Cut				⌘X
Copy				⌘C
Copy Merged				⇧⌘C
Paste				⌘V
Paste Into				⇧⌘V
Clear				
Check Spelling...				
Find and Replace Text...				
Fill...				⇧F5
Stroke...				
Free Transform				⌘T
Transform				▶
Define Brush Preset...				
Define Pattern...				
Define Custom Shape...				
Purge				▶
Adobe PDF Presets...				
Preset Manager...				
Color Settings...				⇧⌘K
Assign Profile...				
Convert to Profile...				
Keyboard Shortcuts...				⌥⇧⌘K
Menus...				⌥⇧⌘M

Pattern Name
Name: Flower   OK   Cancel

Edit	Image	Layer	Select	Filter
Can't Undo				⌘Z
Step Forward				⇧⌘Z
Step Backward				⌥⌘Z
Fade...				⇧⌘F
Cut				⌘X
Copy				⌘C
Copy Merged				⇧⌘C
Paste				⌘V
Paste Into				⇧⌘V
Clear				
Check Spelling...				
Find and Replace Text...				
Fill...				⇧F5
Stroke...				
Free Transform				⌘T
Transform				▶
Define Brush Preset...				
Define Pattern...				
Define Custom Shape...				
Purge				▶
Adobe PDF Presets...				
Preset Manager...				
Color Settings...				⇧⌘K
Assign Profile...				
Convert to Profile...				
Keyboard Shortcuts...				⌥⇧⌘K
Menus...				⌥⇧⌘M

STEP 3

Open a new document or select the shape you want to fill with your new pattern.
Edit > Fill.

STEP 4

A dialogue box will appear. Scroll down to find the Pattern Library.

STEP 5

Click on Custom Pattern to reveal the patterns stored. The last pattern shown will be the one you have just made.

TUTORIAL 12

PHOTOSHOP REPEAT
BLOCK REPEAT WITH
OFFSET FILTER

You can create an easy block repeat by defining your design unit as a pattern. However, if your design is not a simple, flat motif and has texture, you will see a seam appear. By offsetting the design you can carefully mend the seam and avoid any ugly lines passing through the repeat. The mending of a seam can take time and patience, but it is an important part of the process in order to achieve a beautiful and natural pattern.

This tutorial demonstrates a floral painting being put into a repeat. The painting is built up with layers of acrylic paint, and it is critical to maintain the feel and quality of the painting in the mending process.

STEP 1

Filter > Other > Offset.

STEP 2

The Offset palette will appear. Ensure that Wrap Around is selected.
Divide the Horizontal and the Vertical pixel image sizes by two and enter the new values. Click OK.

STEP 3

Your artwork should now be cut into four and flipped so the outsides of the design will match edge to edge. However, seams now run through the design.

STEP 4

Now you need to carefully mend the seams so they merge with the design. You can use any tools that you think appropriate for the job. Here, the Clone tool is used to retain the painted textures. Use a soft brush to avoid creating any hard edges. Paint and draw back into the seams using the Eyedropper tool for colour-matching. You can also copy and paste areas together to build the design up. Keep flattening the artwork as you go if you create any new layers.

STEP 5

Once you are happy with your mending you can offset again (steps one to three) to check the repeat unit.
Finally, flatten the artwork.

STEP 6

Before you define the pattern you can change the unit size.
View > Image Size.

STEP 7

Edit > Define Pattern.

TUTORIAL 13

PHOTOSHOP REPEAT
SIMPLE HALF-
DROP MOTIF

This tutorial shows a simple method for creating a half-drop if you have a motif you wish to put into repeat. As the motif is self-contained, there are no seams to mend and no need to use the more complex method for making a half-drop repeat shown on page 96. You can use this method to create simple patterns that you can store in your Pattern Library.

STEP 1

Open up your motif.
Select > All.
Edit > Copy.

STEP 2

Image > Image Size.
Write down the pixel measurements.

STEP 3

Filter > Other > Offset.
The Offset palette will appear. Ensure that Wrap Around is selected.
Divide the Horizontal and the Vertical pixel image sizes by two and enter the new values. Click OK.

STEP 4

Image > Canvas Size.
Select the middle box on the left-hand side.
For Width, enter 200 percent.

STEP 5

You have already copied the original motif.
Edit > Paste.
Position the new motif next to the first.
Flatten the image.

STEP 6

Change the size of the motif if you wish.
Edit > Image Size.

STEP 7

Edit > Define Pattern.

STEP 8

Open a new document.
Edit > Fill. Find your new pattern.

TUTORIAL 14

PHOTOSHOP REPEAT

HALF-DROP REPEAT

The half-drop is the most complex repeat you can do in Photoshop. The process is straightforward, but you will need patience to mend the seams so that they flow with the design to achieve a fluid repeat. In this tutorial, Victoria Purver's floral painting 'Ophelia' is used to demonstrate a half-drop repeat.

STEP 1

Open your image and flatten the layers.
View > Snap To > All.

STEP 2

Edit > Select All.
Edit > Free Transform.
Notice the crosshairs that appear to mark the central point of your design.

STEP 3

Now drag a ruler so it clicks into place over the crosshairs.
Press Escape.

STEP 4

Select your design. **Edit > Copy**.
Deselect the design.

STEP 5

Image > Canvas Size.
Select the middle square at the bottom.
Change the Height to 200 percent.

STEP 6

Click OK. You will see the canvas size is doubled in height.

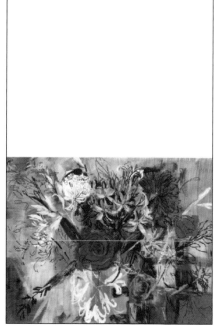

STEP 7

Edit > Paste.
Flatten the image.

Now you need to decide which tools to use to mend the seam; it may be a variety. Here, the Clone tool was used to retain the painted feel of the artwork. Colour-match using the Eyedropper tool, and copy and paste some of the drawn lines. It may help to copy and paste elements from the painting onto the seam. This process is easier and more fluid using a stylus pen. The close-up (near left) shows how the seam was mended by carefully working into the cut area. The Airbrush was used at a variety of opacities to build up subtle layers that mimic the painting technique.

STEP 9

Select > All.
Edit > Copy.
It can help to copy and paste other design elements during the process. For example, the red flower on the far right-hand side was only half an element in the design work and would otherwise have been quite hard to complete using standard Photoshop tools.

STEP 10

Image > Canvas size.
Set the Width to 200 percent so that the canvas doubles in width.

STEP 11

Edit > Paste.
Move the pasted image so the top snaps into place along the guide line.

STEP 12

Duplicate the new pasted layer. Drag this so the bottom snaps onto the guide line. Flatten the layers.

STEP 13

Now mend the seams as before.

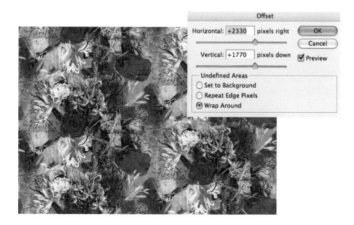

STEP 14

Image > Image Size. Note the pixel size.
Filter > Other > Offset.
Select the Wrap Around option.

STEP 15

Divide the Horizontal and the Vertical pixel image sizes by two and enter the new values. Click OK. New seams will appear that, once again, you will need to mend.

STEP 16

Image > Canvas Size.
Select the middle square at the bottom. Change Height to 50 percent.

STEP 17

Your design is now in a half-drop unit. At this point you may alter the image size. This is the unit that you can give to a digital-print bureau to print out in repeat.

STEP 18

Select > All.
Edit > Define Pattern. Name the pattern.
Open up a new document to see the repeat effect: **Edit > Fill > Pattern**.
Find your new pattern.

TUTORIAL 15

PHOTOSHOP PATTERN
GINGHAM

This tutorial shows how to create the eternally popular gingham pattern. Once created, it can be filled with any colour and changed in scale. It may be used alone or incorporated into a design. However it's applied, it adds a charming, fresh element to a design.

Open a new document in Photoshop at size 5.5 x 5.5 cm (2 x 2 in).

Preferences

Guides, Grid & Slices

Guides
Color: Cyan
Style: Lines

Smart Guides
Color: Magenta

Grid
Color: Custom
Style: Lines
Gridline every: 0.5 cm
Subdivisions: 1

Slices
Line Color: Light Blue
☑ Show Slice Numbers

OK
Cancel
Prev
Next

STEP 2

Adjust your grid settings.
Photoshop > Preference > Guides, Grids & Slices.
A pop-up menu will appear. Set Gridlines to 0.5 cm (¹⁄₅ in), and Subdivision to 1.

STEP 3

View > Show Grid.
View > Snap to Grid.

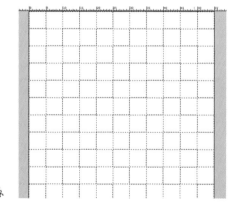

STEP 4

Select the Pen tool from the toolbar. Use the Pen tool to draw alternating squares, using the grid as a guide to create a chequerboard effect. The anchor point should click automatically to the corner point of your grids.

STEP 5

Click on the Paths palette to see the paths you have created.
Click on the Selection icon at the bottom of the palette to make your path a live selection.

Layers | Channels | Paths

Work Path

→ Selection icon

STEP 6

Edit > Fill.
Choose black as the foreground colour.

STEP 7

Bring down horizontal and vertical guide lines 0.5 cm (¹/₅ in) in from the edge of the design.

STEP 8

Use the Pen tool draw a central five-by-five square. Make it into a selection in the Path palette.
Edit > Fill > Foreground Black.

STEP 9

Use the Pen tool again to draw and fill in the corner three-by-three squares and, as before, select them and fill with white.

STEP 10

Now, with your guide lines as your guides and using the Crop tool in the tool palette, crop your design. You have now created the unit for your gingham pattern.

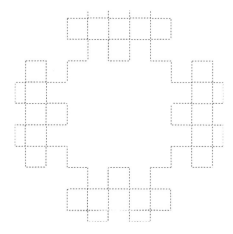

Fill

Contents
Use: Foreground Color ▾

Custom Pattern: ▾

OK
Cancel

Blending
Mode: Normal ▾
Opacity: 80 %
☐ Preserve Transparency

STEP 11

You could now simply select the black and colour it as desired. The following method shows a two-tone effect for a woven look.

Select the gingham and fill with white. Now select it again, and fill with your desired colour. However, change the Opacity in the Fill box to 80 percent.

STEP 12

Use the Pen tool to draw the central square. Select it and fill it with the same colour but with Opacity set to 100 percent. Now your gingham is ready. You can change its size using the Image Size palette to vary the scale.

Fill

Contents
Use: Pattern ▾
Custom Pattern: ▾

OK
Cancel

Blending
Mode: Normal ▾
Opacity: 100 %
☐ Preserve Transparency

Name: Red Gingham

OK
Cancel

STEP 13

Select > All.
Edit > Define Pattern.
Create a new document.
Edit > Fill > Pattern > Red Gingham.

TUTORIAL 16

PHOTOSHOP PATTERN
CREATING STRIPES

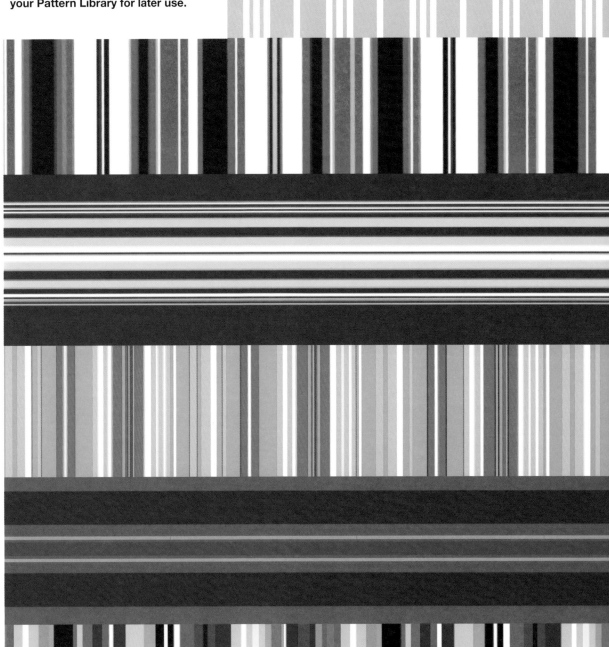

You can create simple or sophisticated stripes in Photoshop and store them in your Pattern Library for later use.

STEP 1

Open a new document. The one shown here is 6 cm x 12 cm (2$\frac{1}{3}$ x 4$\frac{2}{3}$ in).
View > Show Rulers.
Select a long, thin area with the Marquee tool, as shown.

STEP 2

Fill the selected area with colour using the Paint Bucket tool. Continue to build up stripes across the area using this method.

STEP 3

Complete your stripes.
Select > All.

STEP 4

Edit > Define Pattern.
Name your stripe.

Pattern Name

Name: Stripe 1   OK   Cancel

Fill

Contents
Use: Pattern
Custom Pattern:

OK   Cancel

Blending
Mode: Normal
Opacity: 100 %
☐ Preserve Transparency

STEP 5

Open a new document.
Edit > Fill Pattern > Pattern.
Fill the new document with your stripe.

TUTORIAL 17

ILLUSTRATOR REPEAT
BASIC PATTERN
SWATCH

Illustrator offers a simple method of constructing a patterned tile. This tutorial explains how to make a block and half-drop tile that can be used to create striking patterns. Working with vector graphic motifs, you can create a library of pattern swatches to use in designs such as patchwork. You can also create different colour variations.

STEP 1
Create your motif. If it has several elements, group them together.
Edit > Group.

STEP 2
To create a simple block tile, place the motif in the centre of the square, and select both the square and the motif.
Edit > Define Pattern.

STEP 3
To create a half-drop tile, draw a square to place your motif in. Check the View menu and make sure Snap to Point and Smart Guides are selected.

STEP 4
Copy and paste your flower into the square.
View > Outline.

STEP 5
Select the centre of the flower with the Selection tool, and drag it over the left-hand corner of the square. It will snap into place and crosshairs will appear.

STEP 6

Continue until you have completed all the corners, and add a flower in the centre.

STEP 7

View > Preview. Select your filled square.
Edit > Copy > Paste to Back.
With the square still selected, paint it with Stroke and Fill 'none' to create a bounding box. (If you are already using a transparent square, this step is unnecessary.)

STEP 8

Select the square and patterns.
Edit > Define Pattern.
Your pattern will appear in the Swatches palette. Once your swatches are made, save them in the Swatch Library for future use.

STEP 9

Create a shape and fill it with your new swatch tile. Experiment with the Transform tools to change the pattern scale and rotation. Make sure you have the Patterns box selected and Objects and Scale Strokes & Effects deselected.

TUTORIAL 18

ILLUSTRATOR PATTERN
DIAMOND PATTERN

There are an infinite number of ways to create a geometric tile in Illustrator. This tutorial shows how to create a classic diamond pattern. By colouring individual diamond shapes you can build a variety of designs that can be saved in the Swatches palette. Once created in Illustrator, you can save the swatches and use them as pattern tiles in Photoshop.

STEP 1

View > Show Grid.
View > Snap to Grid.
Use the Pen tool draw a diamond with equal sides. The anchor points will snap to the grid.

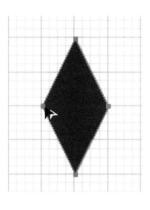

STEP 2

Now go to the View menu and deselect Snap to Grid. Select Snap to Point and Smart Guides instead.

Outline	⌘Y
Overprint Preview	⌥⇧⌘Y
Pixel Preview	⌥⌘Y
Proof Setup	▶
Proof Colors	
Zoom In	⌘+
Zoom Out	⌘–
Fit in Window	⌘0
Actual Size	⌘1
Hide Edges	⌘H
Hide Artboard	
Show Page Tiling	
Show Slices	
Lock Slices	
Hide Template	⇧⌘W
Show Rulers	⌘R
Show Bounding Box	⇧⌘B
Show Transparency Grid	⇧⌘D
Hide Text Threads	⇧⌘Y
Show Live Paint Gaps	
Guides	▶
✓ Smart Guides	⌘U
Hide Grid	⌘"
Snap to Grid	⇧⌘"
✓ Snap to Point	⌥⌘"
New View...	
Edit Views	

STEP 3

Position the pointer on the left-hand anchor point and begin to drag it to the right. Hold down the Shift and Alt keys to constrain and leave a copy.
The cursor will turn white when it has snapped to point.

STEP 4

Repeat this action with the keyboard command Control/Command + D to build up a row of four diamonds.

Here, the pattern has been dropped into a fashion illustration by Daisy Butler.

STEP 5

Once your row of four diamonds is complete, select the top anchor point on the left-hand diamond and, holding down the Option/Alt key, drag it until it snaps into place with the right anchor point of the same diamond. Repeat until you have a row of three diamonds.

STEP 6

Select all the diamonds. Start at the top left-hand diamond's anchor point and, holding down the Option/Alt key, drag it until it snaps into place with the bottom row's left anchor point. Continue to build a fifth row of diamonds.

STEP 7

Select individual diamonds and colour them to create a pattern.

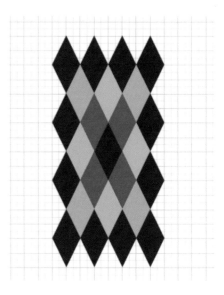

STEP 8

View > Outline.
Window > Attributes.
With all the diamonds selected, click the Show Centre icon to display the centre point of the diamonds.

Show Centre icon

STEP 9

Select the Marquee tool from the Tool palette. Paint it with a Stroke and Fill of 'none'. Draw a rectangle, starting from the centre point of the top left-hand diamond and ending at the centre point of the bottom right-hand diamond.

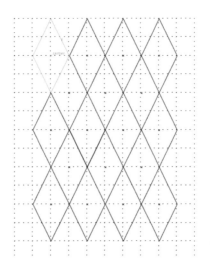

STEP 10

Select the marquee and all the pattern elements.

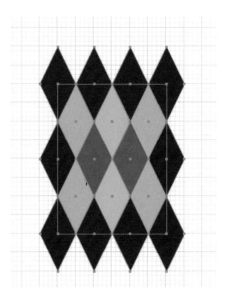

STEP 11

Edit > Define Pattern. Name your pattern and click OK. Your pattern will appear in the Swatches palette.

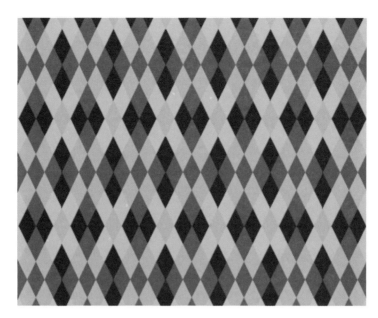

Once you have your diamond unit you can make an infinite number of different diamond formations by selecting and changing the fill colours.

Save each pattern as a swatch, create a rectangle, and fill it with the new swatch patterns to create different effects.

Using the Pen tool, create a diagonal line from the centre points in the outside diamond, and apply a dash to the stroke. This will give a stitched effect reminiscent of the classic Argyle pattern.

PUTTING ILLUSTRATOR PATTERN FILES INTO PHOTOSHOP

Once you have made your pattern tile, save it in the Swatch Library so you can use it again. You can also save it in the Photoshop Pattern Library for use in a Photoshop image.

STEP 1

In Illustrator, open up your saved swatches from the Swatch Library.

STEP 2

Drag your pattern out.
View > Outline.
Select the bounding box.
If the pattern is grouped, **Edit > Ungroup**.
Select the bounding box.
Edit > Copy. Deselect everything.
Edit > Paste in Front.

STEP 3

Select the rectangle.
Object > Crop Marks > Make.
Save the file.

STEP 4

Open up Photoshop and then open your Illustrator file. Alter the resolution to 300 dpi.

STEP 5

Click OK and your pattern tile will open. At this point you can change the Image size. **Object > Image size**.

STEP 6

Select > All.
Edit > Define Pattern.
You can now apply your tiles to a Photoshop file.

TUTORIAL 19

ILLUSTRATOR PATTERN
PLAID PATTERNS

STEP 1

Use the Rectangle tool to create a
1 x 1 cm square (3/8 x 3/8 in).

STEP 2

**Illustrator > Preferences > Smart
Guides & Slices**.
Set the angle to 45 degrees.
Check the View menu to make sure
Smart Guides and Snap to Point are on.

STEP 3

Set Stroke and Fill to 'none'.

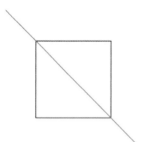

STEP 4

View > Outline Mode.
Select the Pen tool and drag across until
it hits the 45-degree line. Now draw a line
diagonally across the square.
View > Preview.
Give the line a 3 pt black stroke.

STEP 5

Use the Selection tool to grab the diagonal
line. Drag it towards the right-hand corner
of the design, holding down the Shift and
Option/Alt keys to constrain and copy it.
Do not release the mouse button or
the keys until the cursor goes white; this
means it has snapped into place.
Repeat for the left-hand corner line.

STEP 6

Select all three lines to change the
stroke colour.

Edit	Object	Type	Select	Filter
Undo Send to Back				⌘Z
Redo				⇧⌘Z
Cut				⌘X
Copy				⌘C
Paste				⌘V
Paste in Front				⌘F
Paste in Back				⌘B
Clear				

STEP 7

You can alter the colour of the background
and the strokes. Select the three lines and
stroke with a new colour. Select the square
and fill with a new colour.
Select the square.
Edit > Copy.
Edit > Paste to Back.
This will be still selected; paint it with a
Stroke and Fill of 'none'.

New Swatch

Swatch Name: Blue Diagonal

Color Type: Process Color

☑ Global

Color Mode:

C ——————— 0 %
M ——————— 0 %
Y ——————— 0 %
K ——————— 0 %

OK
Cancel

Swatches
Find:

STEP 8

Select > All.
Edit > Define Pattern.
Name your pattern and click OK.
The new pattern tile will appear in the
Swatches palette.

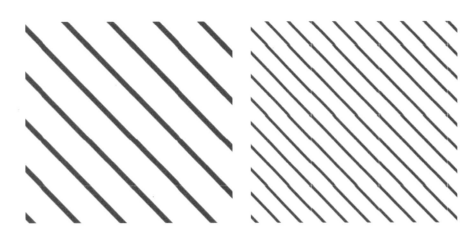

STEP 9

Draw a rectangle and fill it with your swatch. You can change the scale:
Edit > Transform > Scale.
A dialogue box will appear.
Select Patterns. All the other boxes should be deselected.
Now change the Scale percentage.

STEP 10

To build up a basic diagonal plaid:
Edit > Transform > Reflect.
Highlight Vertical with the right-hand pattern box selected, and choose the Copy option.
With this new box selected, lower the Opacity in the Transparency palette to create a weave effect.

STEP 11

Save your swatches to the Swatch Library.

CREATING A PLAID WITH THE DIAGONAL PATTERN TILE

STEP 1

Open a new A4 document. Double-click on the Rectangle tool, and the Measurement dialogue box will open. Enter a measurement of 1 x 29 cm (3/8 x 11 1/2 in). Fill your rectangle with the new diagonal pattern fill.

STEP 2

Select the new rectangle. Press Return and the Move dialogue box will appear. Enter Horizontal Position as 2 cm (4/5 in). Select Object and press Copy. Press Ctrl/Command + D repeatedly to complete the row.

STEP 3

Fill alternate rows with different fills.

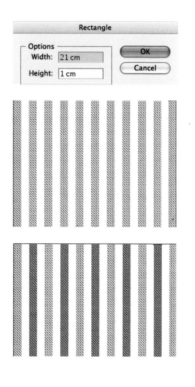

STEP 4

Complete the vertical rows using the same method, but this time enter 2 cm (3/4 in) for Vertical Position in the Move dialogue box.

STEP 5

Select alternate rows and change the Opacity in the Transparency palette to achieve a woven effect.

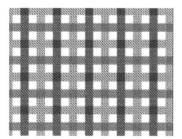

STEP 6

Create a new layer. On this, create a new grid with a fill colour 55 mm (1/5 in) in width.

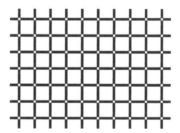

STEP 7

Turn off the top layer to reveal your new check. Select all.
Window > Pathfinder.
Select Exclude Pathfinder, which excludes the overlaps and cuts them away.

STEP 8

Now turn the top layer back on and begin to experiment with colourways by adding a background and changing the colour of the block grid. Try creating other tiles in different colourways for more options.

TUTORIAL 20

ILLUSTRATOR PATTERN
HALF-DROP

This floral design, created in illustrator using various shapes and drawn with a Pen tool, is set inside a square box, which is useful if you wish to make a half-drop repeat.

STEP 1

There is a useful function in Illustrator called Smart Guides. These help to accurately align different grouped objects. Go to the View menu and click on the Smart Guides. A tick should appear next to it to show that it is activated. In addition, click Show Rulers.

STEP 2

Drag some guides down from the ruler bar, until they snap into place on the top and bottom of the square design. It is important to find the centre of the design using the Smart Guides.

STEP 3

To create a half-drop repeat, duplicate the design and align it next to the original so that the box edges are touching and the vertical alignment is on the centre guide.

You can duplicate using the Copy and Paste commands found in the Edit menu, and use the align window found in the Windows menu. Alternatively, select and hold the object with the mouse then press Alt+Shift and drag the object away to automatically duplicate it.

If you drag from the corner edge of the box, the Smart Guides will snap to the edge of the original.

STEP 4

Duplicate and align the design again, as shown in this example.

Drag some vertical guides to snap to the left and right sides of the design. Press **Object > Ungroup** (Ctrl/Cmnd+Shift+G) as many times as possible. This will ungroup all the objects. Delete all the colour boxes and make another box to fit the guide edges.

STEP 6

Copy and paste the box, and choose **Object > Arrange > Send to Back**. Then choose **Object > Lock**. There should be two identical boxes on top of each other. One is locked in position at the bottom of the design and the other is in the exact place but on the top of the design. All you should see at this stage is the colour box with the design poking out from the upper and lower right edges, if you see any other elements of the design, select the box and choose **Object > Arrange > Bring to Front**.

STEP 7

Select the top box and choose **Object > Path > Divide Objects Below**. This will cut the excess design outside of the boxed area. Select and delete the excess design, shown in the example.

You should be left with something similar to this example. Choose **Object > Unlock all** and group all the objects together.

Drag the entire design into the Swatches Window. You will see a small icon resembling the floral design among the other colour swatches.

STEP 10

Test the design by creating a larger box and press the new Swatch icon.
In Chapter Four you will see how to place this half-drop pattern into a fashion Illustration.

CHAPTER 4
INTRODUCTION
TO ILLUSTRATION

INTRODUCTION TO ILLUSTRATION

Textile designers need to present their collections, once designed, in a context that enables others to understand them. This usually means depicting the designs on a garment or an interior. This takes the designs to another level by putting them into a realistic environment and giving the collection a sense of place. Lately the industry has seen the arrival of a wealth of exciting new fashion illustration techniques, due partly to advances in digital technology. This has opened up not just a whole new medium, but also a fresh way to approach the subject.

Illustration is no longer a literal interpretation of textile designs. Instead, illustrators are playing with a world of fantasy and illusion, creating a mood and ambience in which viewers can lose themselves. The sensual and decorative approach that a textile designer has to offer is an excellent starting point. By combining drawing, painting, collage and photography, designers can produce exciting and energetic work that can explore a narrative, giving their design work another dimension.

More often than not the computer is used only as a medium to assemble drawings and design work before collaging them together. The most successful illustrators include some form of personal 'handwriting' in their work. The best starting point is often a sketch, painting or drawing in which the designer experiments with mood and artistic style. Books and magazines can be a great source of inspiration and it is also important for the designer to keep up with trends – not only in fashion but also in graphic styles. Most of your inspiration will tend to come from your original textile collection though, and from this you will probably have established a theme and have already developed an idea of how you want to portray your designs.

Your style of illustration and the media you choose to use will also be influenced by the style of garment for which your designs are intended as well as the weight of the fabric. If your designs are for heavy wools and knits, for example, then you might consider a collage medium to give a sense of weight. Alternatively, if your designs are intended for lightweight silks or chiffons then you could consider working with transparent paint effects to suggest movement and fluidity.

Finally, if you are designing textiles intended for fashion, you will need to develop a style of figure drawing. Most textile designers who are not fashion designers tend to panic at the thought of figure-drawing. But, equipped with their sensual and sensitive drawing skills, they can soon find a confident approach to fashion drawing. A good way to overcome any barriers is through life drawing; developing sketches and line drawings of the figure in various media that can then be drawn upon at a later date. Photography is also a useful medium with which to experiment. Photographs can be traced by hand or digitally and are a helpful way to start an illustration. Tracing should not be considered as cheating, especially for textile designers who are not used to working with the figure. Once you have traced an outline you can apply your own illustrative style as you develop the artwork.

At what stage you apply digital techniques to your illustration is up to you. It may be that you use the computer simply to manipulate and assemble your drawings using Photoshop, or you may wish to give your work the kind of very computerized style that Illustrator can offer.

This chapter includes basic tutorials showing techniques in both Photoshop and Illustrator that you can adapt and develop in your own work to create an individual and personal illustrative style.

Previous page:
This illustration was created by Chae Young Kim for her 'Camouflage Kitchen' dress, the concept being to create a 'future vintage' by giving objects from the 1960s and 1970s a modern expression. After photographing her garment on a mannequin, she superimposed it onto a background created in Photoshop. The images were enhanced with lighting effects and filters.

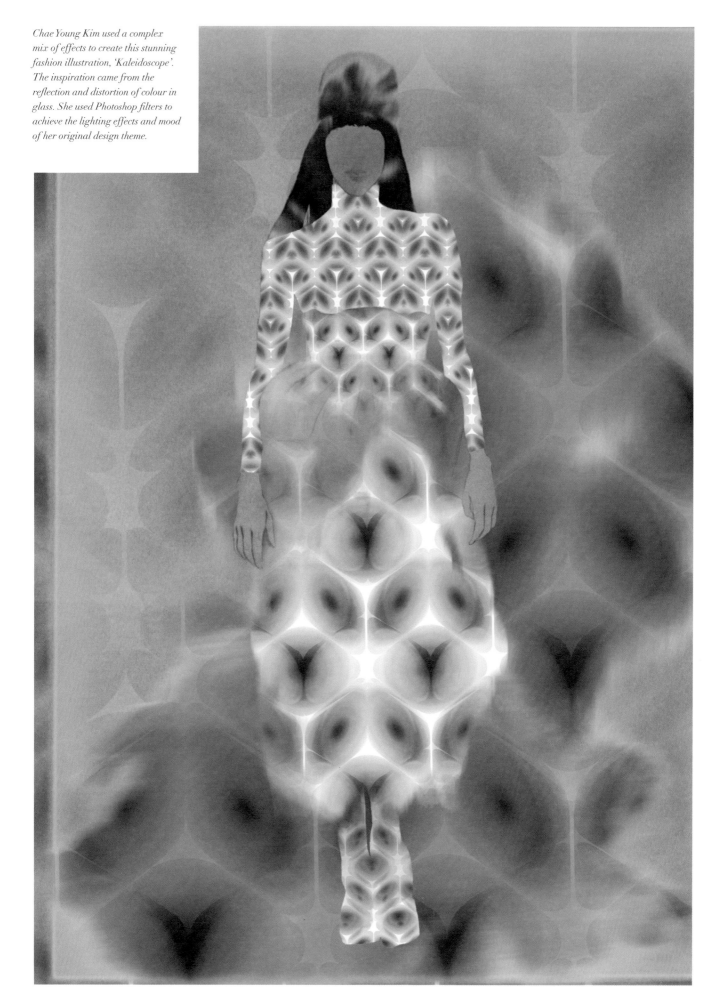

Chae Young Kim used a complex mix of effects to create this stunning fashion illustration, 'Kaleidoscope'. The inspiration came from the reflection and distortion of colour in glass. She used Photoshop filters to achieve the lighting effects and mood of her original design theme.

Amy Isla Breckon places her beautiful hand-rendered drawings in a realistic context. Photoshop allows her to mix drawings and photography to blend the real with the unreal. Here, the combination of an elegant hand-drawn figure with the rustic woodland setting of the photograph creates a dark but sophisticated mood and is perfect for showing off her animal-inspired prints.

Lisa Batchelor illustrated her textile collection for menswear with a strong, graphic style. Initially she worked by hand, creating collages by photographing her textile designs, then cutting them into various garment shapes and collaging them onto black and white photocopied figures. Finally, she scanned them into Photoshop and manipulated them further, adding colour. By maintaining her hand-collaged designs, her illustration has a sense of personal style.

In this magical fashion illustration, Katie Hoppe combined her own decorative line drawings and quirky scanned imagery. She used rich colour and pattern, which she built into an evocative, fairytale mood.

Tolu Ashiru created this fashion illustration by placing a series of pattern swatches that she had created in Photoshop into her bold yet simple fashion drawing.

Pauline Fernandez's rich illustrations evoke the magical and playful mood that she wishes to convey in her designs. Working with a range of photographic imagery, Photoshop allows her to place her designs into a surreal and unusual context. She works with a complex mix of filters and lighting effects to build depth, luminosity and atmosphere. Although her actual textile designs do not dominate here, it does not seem to matter, as the narrative of her illustration cleverly conjures up the mood of her work. This is perhaps more exciting than a literal interpretation.

TUTORIAL 21
TEXTURE-MAPPING
WITH THE PEN TOOL

This tutorial shows how to use the Pen tool to draw around a shape to create a Path template that patterns and textures can then be mapped into. Once a Path has been made it can be saved in the Path palette so that it can be used at any time. This is particularly useful if you want to try adding different effects to a shape, such as applying patterns to furniture, as shown here.

There are two useful Path tools located in the Pen tool in the Tool palette: the Path Selection tool and the Direct Selection tool. The Path Selection tool enables you to move a whole path, and the Direct Selection Tool will let you move a single anchor point.

One you have created a path you can edit it with various other Pen tools, found in the Pen tool's drop-down menu. The Pen tool in Photoshop replicates the Pen tool in Illustrator. It can take a bit of getting used to, but it is worth getting to know and is especially suited to creating Illustrations.

STEP 1

Select the Pen tool from the toolbar. In the option bar, select the Path icon. With the Pen tool, draw around the outside of the chair. Anchor points will be created that can be moved or edited. Draw until you reach the start point to complete the shape.

STEP 2

Go to the Path palette, where you will find your new path. Click on the right-hand arrow and a drop-down menu will appear. Save your path.

STEP 3

You now need to make a new path for the chair's cushion pad.
To create a new path, click on the drop-down menu in the Path palette.

STEP 4

With the Pen tool, draw around the cushion. Save the path as before.

Path Selection tool

STEP 5

Within the path selected, click on the selection icon at the bottom of the Path palette. This will make the path into a live selection.

STEP 6

The selection will be outside the chair; you need to inverse it to select the chair itself.
Select > Inverse.

STEP 7

Open the pattern you wish to paste onto the chair.
Select > All > Copy.
Go to the chair image and, in its Layer palette, select the background layer (with the chairs on). Select your path and the dotted line will appear to define your selection.

STEP 8

Edit > Paste Into.
A new layer will appear.

STEP 9

Edit > Transform.
Use the range of Transform tools to scale, rotate or shear the pattern on the chair to give it perspective. In the Transform tools there is also a Warp tool that will apply a grid around the pattern. By moving the anchor points on the grid you can bend and distort the pattern to create more convincing curves. You will need to experiment with these tools to get the effect you want.

STEP 10

Go to the Path palette, highlight the cushion path and make it into a selection.
Select > Inverse.
Go to your pattern document.
Select > All > Copy.

STEP 11

Go back to your chair image.
Edit > Paste Into.
A new layer will appear. Use the Transform tools to scale and skew the pattern onto the cushion.

STEP 12

To add subtle shadows and highlights you can use the Burn and Dodge tools. The Dodge tool will add highlights, and the Burn tool shadows. Make sure you are on the right layer and select an airbrush from the option bar. With one of the tools selected, carefully move over areas of the chair to create shadows and highlights. Build up shadow on the chair and cushion, making sure to select the right layer.

STEP 13

Continue the same process on the other chairs and paste in new patterns.

STEP 14

Finally, on the background layer, select the black backdrop with the Magic Wand tool and fill it with a pattern from your Pattern Library.

TUTORIAL 22
TEXTURE-MAP AND LINE DRAWING

This tutorial demonstrates how to texture map your design onto a fashion illustration using basic Photoshop tools. The key to fashion illustration is to have a strong vision and create an ambience. Here, Katie Hoppe's design work is inspired by folklore and romantic imagery. Her use of colour is rich, evocative and exotic. She demonstrates how important it is to have a body of original drawings and objects as a palette to work with.

Begin by selecting a fashion image featuring a simple garment that a more complex design can fit into, and create a black-line drawing as a template. You can incorporate other drawings and scanned imagery to give the illustration depth and texture.

STEP 1

Scan your line drawing and open it up in Photoshop.

STEP 2

Image > Adjustment > Brightness and Contrast. Move the sliders to achieve a good definition.

STEP 3

Clean up your image, using the Eraser tool to rub out any stray lines.
Join up any gaps between the outlines in order to make complete shapes to paste your design work into.

STEP 4

Use the Magic Wand tool (tolerance set to 50), to select a section of your black line.
Select > Select Similar.
Select all the black lines.

STEP 5

Edit > Copy. **Edit > Paste**.
A new layer will appear.
Turn the background layer off to reveal your new layer.

STEP 6

Open up your design work.
Select > Select All.
Edit > Copy.

STEP 7

Return to your fashion illustration. Use the Magic Wand tool to select the main part of the dress.
Edit > Paste Into.

STEP 8

A new layer will appear. Use the Move tool to move the design around.
Edit > Transform.
Scale or rotate the design to fit better within the garment.

STEP 9

Go back to the original design and select a section to paste into the sleeves using the Paste Into command. It is important at this stage to manage your layers, as you can end up with too many.

You should have five layers. Turn off the background layer and line-drawing layer. With one of the design layers highlighted, go to the arrow in the top right-hand box and a drop-down menu will appear. Scroll down to Merge Visible to flatten the layers.

Dock to Palette Well

New Layer...   ⇧⌘N
Duplicate Layer...
Delete Layer
Delete Hidden Layers

New Group...
New Group from Layers...

Lock All Layers in Group...

Group into New Smart Object
Edit Contents

Layer Properties...
Blending Options...

Create Clipping Mask   ⌥⌘G

Link Layers
Select Linked Layers

Merge Down   ⌘E
Merge Visible   ⇧⌘E
Flatten Image

Animation Options   ▶
Palette Options...

STEP 10

To incorporate added texture, scan in a sequin trim and open it up in Photoshop.
Select > All.
Edit > Copy.
Return to your fashion illustration with the figure drawing layer selected. Use the Magic Wand tool to select the sleeve.
Edit > Paste into. A new layer will appear. Use the Transform tools to fit your design to the shape of the sleeve. Repeat the process with the other sleeve.

STEP 11

Again, it is important to manage your layers. Turn off the background layer and the line-drawing layer. With one of the design layers highlighted, go to the arrow in the top right-hand box and a drop-down menu will appear. Select Merge Visible to flatten the layers.

STEP 12

You should now have three layers. With the figure drawing layer selected, paint in the figure by making selections with the Magic Wand tool and filling them with colour.

STEP 13

Now the figure is complete. Think about adding a background.

STEP 14

Create a new layer and shift it behind all the other layers.

STEP 17

To create the button tree, scan in a tree-trunk silhouette, select it with the Magic Wand tool and paste it into the background.

STEP 15

Edit > Fill > Foreground colours.
Fill with your chosen colour.

STEP 16

Open up some drawings that you can paste into the background. Here, the bird was selected with the Magic Wand tool and copied and pasted onto the illustration, then coloured in.

STEP 18

Scan in some buttons. Use the Pen tool to carefully draw around the buttons, creating curves around the edges.

STEP 19

Go into the Path palette, and make sure the path you have just created is active by clicking on it to highlight it.
Select the bottom icon to make the path into a selection.
Select > Inverse.

Selection icon

STEP 20

Copy > Paste.
Use the Move tool to arrange the buttons. Duplicate the button layer to build up the button tree.
Merge the button-tree layers to create one layer, as before.

STEP 21

Select and copy some line drawings and paste them into the background. Colour them white and lower the Opacity in the Layer palette to add decoration and ornamentation to the fashion illustration.

TUTORIAL 23

CREATING GRAPHIC SILHOUETTES

This tutorial demonstrates how to place a print design into context for display purposes. The example shows a floral printed design (featured in Chapter Three) being put into a fashion figure illustration.

First you need to create a figure template. The following sequence demonstrates how to trace a figure from a photograph. The required quality of the photo depends on how much detail you wish to trace, but for this exercise you only need to capture the basic form and outline, so a low-resolution image will suffice.

STEP 1

Create a new file in Illustrator, and use the **File > Place** command to import the photograph. Once the photograph has been placed, go to the Layers window on the right and lock the layer. This will prevent the photograph being moved during tracing.

On the same Layers window, create a new layer by selecting the arrow on the right to open the layers command list.

STEP 2

Using the Pen tool, draw around the outline of the figure. You will need some knowledge of using the Pen tool to create and control curves. You will also need to know how to cut paths using the Scissor tool and use the Direct Selection tool to join the paths together (this is to separate the drawing into different sections, ensuring that each section is closed so it can be filled with a colour).

STEP 3

Now create a new layer below the illustration and place a rectangle filled with a colour, to emphasize the illustration.

STEP 4

These examples show how it is possible to add a colour fill to the various sections of the figure. However, the objective here is to focus on the floral pattern, so it is better to create a simple silhouetted figure. When finished, save the illustration.

STEP 5

Open Photoshop and create a new A4 page. Copy and paste the figure separately to the background from Illustrator. It is a good idea to separate elements into different layers. In this case the fashion illustration is separated above the green background. The pattern can be imported into the layer above.

STEP 6

In Photoshop, copy and paste the pattern swatch into the fashion illustration file. It will automatically appear in a new layer above the illustration. The pattern may appear too large to fit on the shirt, so reduce it to the appropriate size with **Edit > Transform** command.

STEP 7

To accurately choose the pattern area, select outside the pattern using the Magic Wand, then choose **Select > Inverse**. Once selected choose **Edit > Define Pattern**. A confirmation window will appear with a thumbnail of the pattern to be defined. If this looks correct, press OK.

STEP 8

Create a new layer and select an area just larger than the section of the target garment.
Choose Edit > Fill.
Another window will appear; choose Pattern on the drop-down menu, and select your design from the thumbnail list. Reduce the opacity on that layer to view the figure behind.

STEP 9

Select the layer with the figure and use the Magic Wand to select the garment area. Go back to the Pattern layer and copy and paste. The pattern cutout will paste into a new layer. Now turn on the Pattern layer to see the results more clearly.

STEP 10

The pattern is now in place, but appears flat. This works with some designs, but here it would be better if it followed the shape and contours of the garment.

Repeat steps 8 and 9, and use the **Edit > Transform > Warp** command to fit the pattern to the garment. It is likely that the garment will need to be fitted in sections – here, the right chest section is warped first, followed by the right arm. The Eraser tool is used to hide the join.

CHAPTER 5
DIGITAL CRAFT

DIGITAL CRAFT

The introduction of new technology in the 21st century is impacting on many different areas of our lives and is developing at such a rapid pace that it is sometimes difficult to keep up. For the new 'digital generation' who are growing up with technology, it has become second nature. But for the designer rooted in traditional processes, it is no longer possible to ignore these new developments in technology. Some see it as a challenge to introduce these new methods into their work, while others are fiercely protective of their tradition and craft.

This chapter looks at whether it is possible for a designer to maintain the 'hand' quality of their work while using new technology. The first part of the chapter, 'Combining old and new', looks at how designers are finding ways to re-introduce traditional hand-crafting skills into their work. The second part, 'Desktop digital textiles', examines how designers are taking advantage of the immediacy and hands-on approach of desktop printing to create a new craft tradition. Should the new skills that are being developed with digital design and print be recognized as a new craft skill, rather than just a mechanical process? This is for you to judge. But the potential for creativity using new technology is clear from the wealth of work shown in this chapter.

Topi Ashiri uses sublimation printing on a variety of unusual polyesters such as aertex and stretch Lycra®. These have been pieced together to make this striking graphic jacket.

COMBINING OLD AND NEW

Working in a virtual environment with a mechanical output seems to make the creator very aware that the personal identity of the work is in danger of being lost. There is also a need for a textile designer to have a physical relationship with the cloth and this can become even more apparent when working in a digital environment.

Many designers are disappointed with the 'flat' outcome of a digital print; the surface and tactile qualities created by traditional print methods are often lost. For some it seems too easy to print at the press of a button without physical effort, and the speed of the digital print process almost seems to compel the practitioner to work extensively on a fabric to slow down the process. The result is that some designers are now finding ways to put back these tactile qualities into the creation of fabric, and into the fabric itself by physical intervention such as over-printing and embellishment.

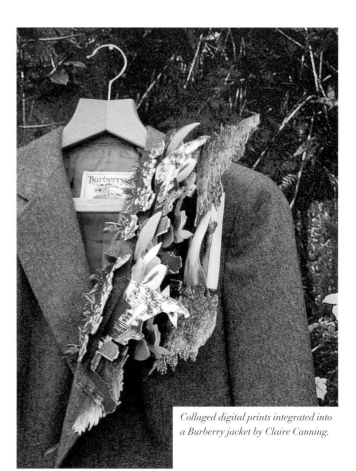

Collaged digital prints integrated into a Burberry jacket by Claire Canning.

Digital printing can appear flat, but once the fabric is made into a garment, it can come to life again. Claire Canning experiments with a combination of traditional screen-printing and digital techniques. She then pushes the potential to create a 3D effect and give her work depth by layering, collaging, bonding and cutting. The rich photographic qualities that can be achieved with digital print give Clare a playful, storybook narrative to her work.

Dominique Devaux creates rich digital prints inspired by her love of jewellery and antiques. She adds metallic foiling to give texture and light.

Melanie Bowles uses sequins and beads on her graphic floral prints to give a 3D effect and offset the flatness of the print.

Leanna Zivanovic's eclectic collection of hand-made cloth dolls was created using a combination of digital printing and screen printing.

This chapter looks at a range of techniques that can be combined with digital print to re-engage the designer with the cloth, in order to create beautiful and innovative surfaces. These range from screen-print methods, such as devoré, discharge print, flocking, foiling and laminating, through dye techniques such as shibori, to fabric manipulation, embellishment and embroidery. Many of these techniques have, until recently, only been explored by couturiers, fashion designers and textile artists due to the cost of digital print.

However, now that many established art institutions have a digital textile print facility, there is a wealth of experimental textile work emerging from art colleges and universities, and professional, small-scale designers are also taking up this newly emerging craft. Much of this work is very experimental and in its early stages of development, but the examples here show the rich effects that can be achieved.

HAND PAINTING AND DIGITAL PRINT

Hand painting or drawing onto fabric is the most immediate method of adding depth to a digital print. Because of its simplicity this technique is sometimes ignored, but its spontaneity can complement the mechanical process of digital printing and also make the design much more personal. There are many fabric pens available that can produce a very good effect, including glitter, pearlized and puff pens.

Zoe Barker scans her beautiful floral paintings and then prints them digitally onto silk. She further paints into the fabric by hand to add an extra layer to her work.

Dominique Devaux's collection, 'Exotic Paradise', is based on her love of exotic birds and florals and inspired by childhood memories of the Caribbean. The qualities of light and reflection have been created by embellishing the fabrics with hand-painted foil glitter. This has brought the digital print to life and gives an individual and glamorous edge to her work. Bands of brightly-coloured silks give a contemporary and exotic appeal, and the juxtaposition of real jewellery, sewn over photographic images of the same jewellery, adds another layer. The result is a highly effective, sensitive and sensual approach to digital design.

SCREEN PRINTING AND DIGITAL PRINT

Screen printing is a fast method of working into a digital print using traditional print techniques; colour is positioned in a design using screens. There are several chemical recipes for silk-screening, and the most suitable ones for combining with digital print are: pigment printing, devoré, discharge printing and the application of adhesive for flocking and foiling. The screen print has to work not only in harmony with the design, but also within the limitations of the fabric and print-quality. Achieving the desired results can take much testing to achieve, and you will need a good knowledge of print techniques and an awareness of the health and safety issues involved.

Here, Emamoke Ukeleghe digitally printed a design of text with a hand-drawn pattern onto cotton satin, and then used a screen-print method to overprint with peach pigment.

As a designer, Ukeleghe crosses between the textile traditions of Nigeria and east London. She merges digital techniques with traditional techniques to create a fusion between old and modern, ethnic and Western. In the above bag on the right, entitled 'Purpose, Wisdom and Enlightenment', she digitally printed stripes onto cotton drill and then overprinted broken stripes in peach. In the bag on the left, 'Laces', she made a large-scale drawing of shoelaces with black ballpoint pen, which she then digitally printed onto cotton.

In her powerful textile collection, 'Belonging(s)', Ukeleghe uses digital print combined with pigment screen-printing. Her inspiration came from issues surrounding displacement, and each piece tells a personal story. Here, a circular pattern was digitally printed onto cotton satin then overprinted with blue and white pigments. By including a photograph of a family member, she integrates a personal memory into her work.

DEVORÉ AND DIGITAL PRINT

Devoré printing involves the burning out of one of the fibre blends of cellulose-protein fabrics such as silk/viscose mix. Once the chemical devoré paste is applied it will burn away one of the fibre types to leave a transparent area. Many digital-print bureaus supply pre-treated fabric specifically for the devoré process, such as silk/viscose satin and silk/viscose velvet. The chemical paste is applied to the fabric, either by hand- or by screen printing, in the areas that are to be burnt away. This can be done after digital printing has taken place. A heat process is then used to burn away the pattern areas to reveal a sheer, translucent area of fabric. The devoré process is time consuming and labour intensive, but the results can be beautiful. It should be approached with caution and health and safely guidelines followed as strong chemicals are used in the process.

Once the fabric has been put through the devoré process, the base colour of the fabric is revealed. This area can be cross-dyed to re-introduce colour into the cloth. Cross-dyeing works well with the devoré process as it stands out on the fibre that has not been burnt away. If you used a screen to apply the devoré paste, you can use the same screen to apply the cross-dye.

Louisa-Claire Fernandes' dramatic furnishings collection, 'Simplexity', combines digital and screen-printing techniques. First she created a digital print that became a background on which she applied other techniques. A large-scale devoré print gave her work a luxurious quality, and the dip-dyed effect was created by scanning in hand-painted papers. Her work demonstrates the combination of mechanical- and hand processes to create a 'new fabric' couture-furnishing collection.

Devoré paste has been silk-screened onto the digital print. Once the paste is dry, heat was applied with an iron or heat press to burn out the viscose and leave the silk.

Louisa-Claire Fernandes used a large-scale digital print onto a silk/viscose mixed fabric. The devoré area was cross-dyed in turquoise.

FOILING AND FLOCKING WITH DIGITAL PRINT

Foiling and flocking onto a digital print are popular choices for highlighting and embellishing designs. They are not as risky as the more experimental processes such as devoré and discharge printing, which are time consuming and complicated. Flocking gives a beautiful raised texture to the surface of a fabric, which is often lacking with digital printing. Foiling can give highlights and added sparkle to a fabric, especially when the fabric moves.

Metallic foils come in a variety of jewel colours as well as metallic effects such as copper, gold and silver, and can be bought in sheet form from craft suppliers. Iridescent and holographic foils are also available.

In foiling, water-based or solvent adhesive is either applied through a screen or hand-painted onto the fabric. A sheet of foil is then stuck onto the adhesive. Heat is applied with an iron or heat-press and, once the foil has cooled, the sheet is peeled back to leave behind a foiled area.

Small areas of foiling can be added to a digital print to highlight areas and make them glitter. You can also use a clear 'foil' to create matt and shiny areas on a fabric that catch the light when the fabric moves. Carefully consider where to apply the foil so that the design and the foiling effect work together.

The raised, 'velvet' effect of flocking is traditionally associated with decorative wallpapers. However, it is also suitable for fashion fabrics and can add a luxurious surface to the cloth. Flock can be purchased on a roll, attached to a backing paper. It is usually supplied in white, but it may be hand-coloured with dyes. Flocking paper can be digitally printed onto a Mimaki digital printer and then applied onto a fabric, but this is still an experimental process.

Similar to the foiling process, the flocking paper is placed (flock-side down) onto a glued area. Heat is applied using an iron or a heat-press and, once cool, the backing paper is peeled back to reveal the flocked area.

Amelia Mullins applied bold areas of gold foiling to complement her digitally-printed silk dress.

Charlotte Arnold creates intriguing surface effects by applying digital flocking onto digitally-printed silk. The result is a 'new' looking fabric with a mixture of photographic imagery, light and texture

Georgina Papandreou applied foil to her geometric digital print to create a fractured, 3D lighting effect. The effect interplays with the printed design as well as with the surface of the fabric, giving the work a rich texture.

Emily House's 'Plastic Maze' was digitally printed onto cotton poplin and then plastic-laminated and edged with a reflective trim.

Matthew Williamson's S/S 05 collection features this 'Rainbow Dress' – digitally-printed chiffon embellished with metallic foil.

DESIGNER PROFILE: PATRICIA BELFORD

'Spoons' – vintage urban scene digitally printed onto disposable plastic spoons (UJV digital printer).

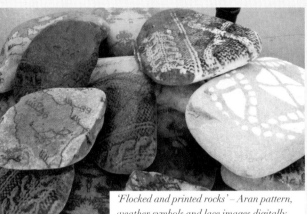

'Flocked and printed rocks' – Aran pattern, weather symbols and lace images digitally printed and hand-flocked onto rocks (UJV digital printer, hand flock print).

Patricia Belford, originally from Northern Ireland, created Belford Prints in 1986. Belford's became known for innovative and creative use of print techniques for fashion and furnishing designers, and its clients included Vivienne Westwood, Jasper Conran, Zandra Rhodes, Neisha Crosland and The Designers Guild. The business developed from being a company based on textile techniques, and by 2004 had become focused on menswear and digital printing.

The arrival of commercial digital print in 1999 was a huge boost for the print- and fashion industries, opening them up to almost anyone who wanted to print without the time and expense of creating screens. But Belford felt that her skills as a creative textile designer were being swamped by the digital explosion. As a hand textile printer, she found the results of digital printing to be somewhat lacking in depth.

In 2005, looking for new challenges, Belford took up a position as a Senior Research Fellow with Interface (Fabric Forward) at the School of Art and Design at the University of Ulster. Located in

'Contemporary circles' – a range of ideas from the contemporary souvenir project display in circles (TX3 digital cloth printer, UJV digital printer, laser cutter, digital stitch, hand flock and hand foiling).

'Felt lace' – felted fabric laser-cut with a design from the Carrickmacross Archive held at The Ulster Folk Museum, Northern Ireland (laser cutter).

Northern Ireland, a region of renowned textile tradition, Fabric Forward builds upon a record of excellence in textile research. Utilizing the extensive print facilities of Interface – UJF ultra violet hard surface digital printer, Mimaki TX3 digital printer, laser cutter, long-arm quilter, digital-stitch and traditional hand-print table – the results are evidence that traditional and digital disciplines combined can create innovative results.

At Fabric Forward, Belford has found a creative side to digital print and has been responsible for the implementation of two exciting projects bridging the digital and the traditional: 'Contemporary Souvenir' and 'Reinventing Linen'.

The 'Reinventing Linen' project explored the realistic workings of high- and low tech, referencing traditional methods while embracing contemporary technologies. Part of the focus for this piece was the poem 'The Linen Industry' by renowned Belfast poet Michael Longley. The poem was digitally printed, woven, flocked, stitched and foiled to produce a seven-metre long piece of art (below).

'Poem': the full seven-metre (23- foot) length of the artwork.

'Poem' detail: digitally printed and woven dress with addition of hand flocking and digital stitch.

'Poem' detail: digitally printed and woven shirt section with digital stitching.

RESIST DYEING AND DIGITAL PRINT

Resist dyeing techniques – such as tie-dye, batik and shibori – are among the oldest textile-dyeing techniques. They are used all around the world and are still a source of fascination to many artists and designers today.

Shibori is the collective Japanese term for tie-dye, stitch-dye, fold-dye and pole-wrap-dye techniques, which have also been used for centuries as a textile craft all over the world. Chinese in origin, it has been used in Africa, the Middle East and India, and is still used today. The method ranges from simple resist techniques to advanced methods of shibori in which complex layers of colour are built up. Shibori creates not only 2D patterns, but can also create 3D fabrics when the folding and wrapping used to achieve the resist areas is left in the cloth.

An element of surprise is always present in the making of shibori cloth, which contributes to its special magic and popularity, and can be used complement the mechanical processes of digital printing.

Textile designer Stacey Wickens first explores the shibori technique by hand. She then scans samples into the computer and drops them into floral shapes, which she arranges using imaging software before printing them digitally onto silk satin. The dark background enhances the beauty of this ancient technique.

Stacey Wickens experiments by reversing the technique, first printing large-scale versions of floral motifs digitally onto silk satin and then applying shibori on top. By using a simple but bold motif in her digital design, she maintains a balance between the two processes.

EMBROIDERY, EMBELLISHMENT AND DIGITAL PRINT

In recent years there has been a revival of the traditional crafts of knitting, crochet and embroidery. In a world dominated by technology, many people enjoy creating garments and accessories by hand and returning to traditional techniques. At the same time, there has been a resurgence in the popularity of vintage garments and embellishments, which has also encouraged designers to look back at traditional techniques of hand- or machine stitching to add interest, value and individual style to their own designs.

Today, designers are combining the traditional techniques of embroidery and embellishment with digital print to add a 'hand-crafted' element to their textile designs. If carefully applied, the two skills can complement one another.

Emma Rampton's textile collection 'Second Life', consists of multifunctional garments that are designed to have a second life. The wearer is allowed to customize and interact with the garment as time goes on. Working with contemporary and traditional imagery from domestic life, she combines new technology with traditional stitch techniques, worked back into the fabric.

Dominique Devaux's love of vintage textiles provides inspiration for her design work. In her collection 'Exotic Paradise', she sewed vintage embroidered sections onto her digital prints. The printed fabric echoed the real embroidered motif to create a 'modern antique' look.

Katie Irving Jones draws stitchwork patterns inspired by historic embroideries. She then scans and further manipulates them using imaging software. She prints her designs digitally onto a cotton/linen mix to give the effect of canvas work. Finally, she hand-stitches back into the motifs to give a personal, hand-crafted touch to the fabric.

Andrea Patterson combines appliqué, stitch and trimmings such as lace, buttons and ribbons. She demonstrates her use of digital print and design techniques with hand detailing to the fabric and garment.

Photini Anastasi's digital collection retains her beautiful and sensitive drawings and watercolour paintings of landscape scenes from her childhood. She prints digitally onto viscose satin and then hand embroiders back into the images, imitating the lines and marks of her drawings.

DESIGNER PROFILE: HELEN AMY MURRAY

British-born textile designer Helen Amy Murray is an emerging talent, creating beautiful, luxury one-of-a-kind textiles for interiors and wallcoverings. Murray was educated at Chelsea College of Art, London. In 2003 she won the prestigious Oxo Peugeot Design Award, as well as a prize for innovation from the National Endowment for Science, Technology and the Arts (Nesta). She then set up her own label, HelenAmyMurray, and has exhibited her work internationally.

'Birds and Flowers' (2005) – An ambitious art piece printed onto silk satin into which Murray hand-sculpted. Initially working and adapting her design using imaging software, she dropped in colour blends and gradients, then printed the artwork digitally. Drawing back into the design with her cutting tool to create a 3D effect, she gave further detail, definition, shadow, movement and depth to the piece. Finally, she framed it in timber covered with foiled leather.

At Chelsea, Murray developed a passion for creating 3D surface effects on various fabrics such as silk, leather and suede. She has since developed a technique that has been recognized internationally for its unique hand-crafted construction. She explains, 'I'm excited about fabric manipulation and using innovative techniques, beautiful luxury materials and design to create couture for the high end of the market.'

Murray's inspiration comes from forms found in nature, from which she creates complex pattern structures using her unique technique. Her work achieves a strong graphic look; her innovative process creating sophisticated 3D fabrics.

The designer's work originates from her love of working directly with the surface of fabrics, so when she decided to take the bold move of exploring digital design she discovered a completely new way of working. 'At first I felt nervous working in a virtual medium. As I have a very physical and tactile relationship with fabric, I felt I was entering the unknown. But once I had completed the process of designing and digitally printing and had applied my technique, I could see the possibilities that it would give my work. I love the subtlety of colour that digital print can achieve and the layers of pattern and form. It allows me to work with more complex and fantasy imagery that gives my work a new narrative.'

Murray's highly individual and sensual approach to textiles allows her work to develop without compromising her aesthetic values. She has merged digital print so well with her own cutting techniques that she has managed to create a truly 'digitally crafted' textile.

'Art Deco Chair, Two-headed Bird with Sunrays' (2005) – Murray integrated a digitally-printed piece into her sculpted leather fabric, which was then upholstered onto a classic Art Deco chair. She scanned her hand-drawn image of an exotic crane, which she then adapted using imaging software. This was then digitally printed onto silk crêpe satin and carefully appliquéd onto the leather before she applied her cutting process. The digital print on silk satin allowed her to introduce an intricate gradient of colour, adding depth and movement.

PRE-TREATMENT OF DIGITAL FABRIC

All fabrics used for digital printing must be pre-treated before use. The Textile Environment Design (TED) project at the Chelsea College of Art and Design, London, looks at the role the designer can play in creating textiles that have a reduced impact on the environment, and provides a toolbox of designer-centred solutions. Part of the resource offered by TED investigates the coating of organic fabrics so that they are suitable for digital printing, such as organic cottons, linens and hemp. These fabrics were specially coated by a digital-print bureau. Melanie Bowles has created a collection, 'Material Attachment', that is digitally printed onto a hemp/silk mix, proving that rich and vibrant colours can be achieved. The use of organic hemp/silk introduces a new fabric for digital print that has a beautiful surface and subtle sheen.

In her collection 'Material Attachment', Melanie Bowles drew inspiration from historical textiles. The collection was shown at 'Ever & Again' at Chelsea College of Art and Design in 2007, an exhibition which looked at recyling textiles. Melanie re-lined a favourite coat with digitally-printed organic hemp/silk mix fabric to give it a new lease of life.

Nicky Gearing and Debbie Stack from the London College of Fashion experimented with the pre-treatment process as part of an international research project with the Creative Industries Faculty at Queensland University of Technology in 2004. This was a design exercise featuring reworked vintage clothing dating from the nineteenth and twentieth centuries donated by Queensland National Trust. Gearing and Stack screen printed the pre-treatment paste – consisting of sodium carbonate, Manutex and urea – onto an original Victorian damask. The vintage fabric took the inks successfully and withstood the after-treatment of steaming and washing well. They produced an interesting range of samples on various fabrics, integrating discharge and screen-printing techniques with digital print. Digital embroidery was applied to the fabric before the pre-treatment, and also as a final embellishment after printing to create a rich surface quality. The project resulted in a collection of fabrics that show the potential of pre-treatment on fabrics not normally used for digital print.

Digital print onto vintage damask appliquéd onto a traditional ticking cotton and combined with screen printing.

Digital floral print onto dyed ticking fabric combined with discharge printing.

DESKTOP DIGITAL TEXTILES

The rise of mass production and consumerism has led to a craft-focused backlash and more people are now interested in DIY design-and-make. Amateurs are finding ingenious ways to personalize and customize their own products – and not just in the domestic arts, but in graphic design, journalism and publishing, too.

You no longer have to be a trained graphic designer to create personal graphics such as business cards, logos, mouse mats, greetings cards and simple websites. Imaging software is now available as a design tool for all to use and the desktop printer has developed into a key method of print-production for all kinds of graphic materials. Craft enthusiasts are now embracing the hands-on digital technology that is available from the home, and this extends to textiles, primarily through inkjet transfers and sublimation printing.

Rachel Boxall designed these inventive 'Stitch Me' craft kits using imaging software and produced them on her desktop printer. She liked the idea of making a DIY kit following a traditional pattern but using new technology. Rachel created a series of compositions from her drawings and scanned them. She then printed them out by feeding embroidery canvas through her desktop printer. (This does have risks attached to it as stray threads can dislodge the print heads. A safer method is to apply the design with a transfer.)

Andrea Patterson prints her designs onto opaque transfer paper and then applies it to contrasting cotton muslin. The 'plastic' quality of the opaque transfer adds texture and contrasts with the coarseness of the natural muslin.

Kim Chin created her inventive collection of handmade characters from household fabrics such as cleaning cloths, felt, ribbons and plastic. She uses low-tech printing techniques such as sublimation printing with a desktop printer. This use of digital printing onto unusual backgrounds adds to the quirkiness of the collection.

INKJET TRANSFERS

The simplest and most direct method of inkjet printing onto fabric is by running inkjet-transfer paper through a printer and then applying the pattern onto fabric using heat, either with an iron or, ideally, in a heat-press. The paper is a special polymer-treated paper which is manufactured for use as a T-shirt transfer, and is available from stationery and computer suppliers. It is designed for use with water-based inks. In the past the paper left a 'plastic' feel to the fabric, but now a softer result can be achieved. It works best on white or pale fabrics, but there is also an opaque paper available that can be used on darker fabrics, though this will leave a plastic feel.

This simple method of printing, which can be done using most desktop printers, has created a surge in DIY design and print for the amateur craft and hobby sector. Adults and children alike are enjoying this hands-on and immediate approach to transferring images onto mouse mats, jigsaws, coasters and clothes.

Of the 'craft' hobbyists, it is perhaps the quilter who can find the most creative potential in this method of printing. It is possible to apply a non-toxic chemical formula to a fabric to make the image permanent. This is applied by first soaking the fabric in the solution and, once dry, ironing it onto freezer paper. The fabric can then be fed through the printer. Quilters require small, sample-sized amounts of fabric to work with, and, using the inkjet transfer technique, they can create many individual designs to incorporate into their work. Added to this is the tradition of a quilt as a valued artefact that is passed down from one generation to the next. Using this new technology, they can include photographic imagery in their work, adding a highly personalized and powerful sentimental quality to the quilt, which is changing the aesthetic of the craft.

In 'Fragmented Bell' (opposite page, bottom left), the bell-like dress was originally hand stitched by the employees of the Children's Home of Cincinnati. The panoramic image of the piece references natural disasters – in this case digital images of a tornado. Textile artist Shelly Goldsmith digitally manipulated the photograph in order to fragment the plane of the image to reference the actual fragmentation of the domestic landscape.

Goldsmith used reclaimed christening dresses to create 'Baptism'. (opposite page, right). The dress references the use of water in the christening ceremony, while also commenting on how these garments are handed down and reused over many years. As in 'Fragmented Bell', the dress shows the image of a natural disaster and raises the notion that cloth retains a type of memory that cannot be erased. The gown has been transfer-printed with digitally adjusted photography, carefully pieced together to create a panorama-effect around the garment.

Zoe Barker uses the inkjet transfer method to build up complex fabrics for her childrens collection, 'Second Life'. She encourages the children to interact with the clothes and appreciate their worth with her 'customizing kit', containing transfers, badges, buttons and ribbons, which can be added to personalize the garments.

Patchwork entitled 'When I Sleep I Dream of Play'. Alice Potter enjoys the immediacy of translating her designs from sketchbook to fabric via her desk-top printer. She produces small fabric samples that she then pieces together to create patchworks.

The technique of transfer printing is used by aforest-design to present a limited edition of odori tabi socks designed by Sara Lamusias. The tabi is a traditional sock from Japan that is used in the home or is worn with sandals. These photo-collage designs are transfer-printed onto cotton socks.

Textile artist Shelly Goldsmith creates her poignant textile pieces using her desktop printer to print digitally onto transfer paper. She meticulously jigsaws her images together by hand and irons them onto fragile, reclaimed garments. Collaging her images allows her to maintain a hand-crafted quality to her work.

SUBLIMATION PRINTING

Dye-sublimation printing is a versatile method of printing using disperse dyes, – available in cartridge form for large-format printers and for desktop printers – onto polyester fabrics. It is widely used in the promotional marketing industry for printing products such as jewellery, place mats, marble, ceramic tiles or mugs, skateboards, aprons and other items of apparel. The majority of products printed using this process are somewhat crude in design, but there is huge potential to develop more sophisticated work. Many designers are now exploring this method of print, not least because the transfers yield stunning and beautiful photorealistic results, with vivid colours.

There is a wide range of polyesters available from fabric stores. These range from novelty fabrics to satin to metallic lamé and from stretch-knit jerseys to Lycra®. The affordability of these fabrics gives scope for the textile designer to experiment. Some fantastic results can be achieved with the vivid, clear colours of polyester.

In the textile industry, sublimation printing has mainly been used for printing on sportswear and swimwear. However, setting up a desktop print system is now proving to be an affordable option, and many textile designers, studios and educational establishments are now exploring the possibilities of sublimation printing onto the large variety of polyester fabrics that are available. The choice of polyesters can range from aertex, polymesh, lamé, satin, Lycra®, organza and fleece to an array of novelty fabrics, but the higher the percentage of polyester that they contain – preferably more than 60 percent – the better the results. It is always best to test fabrics as many do not state the proportion of polyester that they contain.

Taina Lehtinen's handbag collection was created using sublimation printing onto faux suedette, showcasing the fantastic photographic qualities that can be achieved with this process.

Chetna Prajapati created a beautiful pleated fabric by first printing a metallic polyester using the dye-sublimation technique. She then applied a pleating template and heat-pressed the fabric into shape.

Chetna Prajapati pushed the potential of sublimation printing to create her edgy streetwear collection, 'One Tribe, One Style'. Taking inspiration from contemporary youth culture and the traditional crafts of Africa and North America in the 1980s, she mixed the two to create an eclectic collection. She printed on a range of polyesters, combining them to create her garments. The quality of the colours and definition of the digital print is so strong that some colours look fluorescent; the metallic polyesters add sharpness to the graphic geometric designs.

Victoria Collins tests a wide range of polyesters, such as neoprene and Lycra®, before bonding them together to create new surfaces. Her sketchbook demonstrates the importance of testing different fabrics. She finds that most need to be heat-pressed for 60 seconds at 180C, but care must be taken with nylon as it can melt quickly under a heat-press.

In the past, polyester has been uncomfortable to wear and lacked the qualities of natural fabrics such as cotton. Recently, however, a number of manufacturers have come up with new processes that have resulted in soft, breathable and comfortable fabrics. Polyester is also inexpensive, allowing designers the freedom to experiment with this hands-on method to create innovative print effects. Samples can be produced immediately, which is perfect for the ever-increasing pace of the fashion industry, where ideas need to be realized instantly.

Using the Epsom 3000 desktop printer, Tolu Ashiru demonstrated the possibilities of sublimation printing on her bomber jacket. She printed onto a mix of Lycra®, knit, aertex and elastic, and laminated the plastic collar. Customization, unusual fabrics and bold graphics give her fashion collection a streetwear/sportswear look.

DESIGNER PROFILE: REBECCA EARLEY

Rebecca Earley is a lecturer in Textile Environment Design (TED) at Chelsea College of Art and Design, London. She is an award-winning fashion textile designer who produces textiles for her own label, B.Earley, which she set up in 1995 with backing from the Crafts Council and the Prince's Trust. A practice-based design researcher, her work encompasses a wide range of design-related activities including producing digitally-printed textiles for her own label, undertaking public art projects and commissions and acting as an educator, facilitator and curator.

Earley graduated from Central Saint Martins in 1994 and her graduate collection was widely recognized as groundbreaking. The heat-photogram print technique that she pioneered has since become an industry-standard printing process.

Rebecca Earley's collections demonstrate how the designer can work fluently with digital technology and handcrafted techniques. She retains the original handcrafted look of the heat-photogram process, in which she paints disperse dyes directly onto transfer paper, places a real object directly onto the paper and applies heat to transfer the image onto polyester. Now working digitally, she scans in the original photogram artwork and then rearranges it using imaging software. This gives her the scope to change the scale and composition of her artwork, and more freedom to experiment. Her designs are printed out on a desktop printer using sublimation printing.

In the collection featured here, shirts have been created and delicately embellished with stitched- and pleated details inspired by research into traditional English gardening attire and images of old garden artefacts. Earley uses the digital process as another tool to integrate into her creative process.

This 'Digital Photogram Collage' was created using heat-photogram prints on fabric, which was then digitally scanned and manipulated and digitally printed.

Rebecca Earley, 'Top 100', 2002–08. Heat Photogram..

In 1998, Earley's interest in the environment prompted her to analyze her own studio design and production practices. She subsequently developed an exhaust printing technique that produced hand-printed textiles with no water pollution and minimal chemical usage. She has continued to investigate new techniques and theoretical approaches to textile design, working on a variety of projects, including: Natural Indigo at the Eden Project; Well Fashioned, an exhibition of eco-fashion at the Crafts Council Gallery; Ever & Again: Rethinking Recycled Textiles, an AHRC- (Arts & Humanities Research Council) funded three-year project; Top 100, a long-term polyester-shirt recycling project.

In 2002 Earley joined the Textiles Environment Design (TED) project – a research project where staff and students work collaboratively and on individual projects. This unique research cluster seeks to explore the role that the designer can play in producing more environmentally-friendly textiles. TED places the designer, rather than the manufacturer or consumer, centre-stage, since '80–90 percent of total lifecycle costs of any product (environmental and economic) are determined by the product design before production ever begins' (*More for Less*, Design Council Report, 1998).

TED has developed a series of environmentally-friendly principles and possible strategic solutions, which include: minimizing waste; using less harmful substances, energy and water; utilizing new low-impact technologies; designing systems and services to support textile products; creating long- or short-life textiles. In the last four years the social and cultural awareness and concern for the environment has grown exponentially, and Rebecca and TED have played a key role both nationally and internationally in creating and promoting eco textile design.

Left: Heat photogram, 'Pin Print', 1995; Middle and right: both 'The Conscious Gardener', 2007, combining digital and sublimation printing with hand-painted transfer techniques.

CHAPTER 6
TECHNOLOGY FOR
DIGITAL TEXTILE
PRINTING

Digital inkjet printing is an increasingly important process within the industry, both as a mechanism for 'sampling' printed designs as well as being a full production tool. Digital printing allows virtually any image quality to be printed but does have its limitations, which are outlined within this chapter. However, it is important to recognize that it is printing processes themselves that have been responsible for many of the visual 'languages' or styles that we see in textile design, and having an understanding of the technologies involved is key to appreciating this. This knowledge allows more control over the final result as well as the ability to create cutting-edge work. This chapter opens with a summary of the traditional technologies involved in textile printing, and examines digital textile printing in detail.

TRADITIONAL TEXTILE PRINT TECHNOLOGY

In order to understand the advantages of digital textile printing, it is important to comprehend the preceding technologies. Most traditional methods of printing textiles (as well as other media) are based on processes that use a template as a method for transferring a design onto the substrate. The techniques described here explain the basic categories of traditional textile printing techniques.

Relief Printing: a pattern is carved into wood or another material, as in woodblock printing.

Gravure or Intaglio: a process of incising marks into the surface, usually metal, as in copper plate printing.

Stencilling: a positive/negative process, as in rotary screen and hand silk-screen printing.

Heat Transfer: when dye is transferred from paper to fabric using heat, as in sublimation printing.

Photoprinting: where an image is broken down into four colours, namely cyan, magenta, yellow and black (CMYK), and printed out as a series of small dots, as in four-colour process printing.

WOODBLOCK PRINTING

Block printing is an ancient method for printing images onto fabric. It is generally associated with woodblock printing, but there are examples of blocks being made from terracotta or metal. An image is carved into the wood to create a relief of the design and then pressed into colourant. The ink that remains on the surface of the block is then transferred to fabric by pressure. The blocks could range from a simple small motif using only one colour to complex and large-scale blocks that required stamina and skill on behalf of the printer. The blocks are registered by pin marks that the printer lines up with each repeat of the block. This was the main process for printing textiles in 19th-century England.

Woodblock prints on silk crêpe and linen c. 1930-50 by Joyce Clissold. Shown alongside are some of the original woodblocks.

GRAVURE PRINTING

Gravure printing is a method that first appeared in Europe in the mid-18th century. Initially this process involved images being incised into a metal plate (usually copper) and dye applied to the whole surface. The plate is then scraped, leaving the dye within the incised lines remaining. This allows the pattern to be transferred to the cloth by using pressure. Great skill in using linear marks and cross hatchings developed within the textile industry and the most famous examples became known as 'Toile de Jouy'. A distinct visual language emerged with this print process and it is often referenced in contemporary textile design today.

'Toile de Jouy' gravure printed image from the V&A Museum collection.

ENGRAVED ROLLER PRINTING

With increasing interest in mechanization in the 18th- and 19th centuries, eventually the metal plate became a metal roller. This allowed the speed of printing to increase as well as new processes for transferring designs onto the metal, creating new design possibilities that allowed a fuller range of colours to be used. The ability to use halftone process or continuous tones or colours further enlarged the range of images that could be printed.

STENCILLING

All screen printing works on the principle of a stencil and the use of positive and negative imagery. Stencilling involves isolating each colour found in an image as a positive or negative shape, defined by colour boundaries. Holes defined by the area for each shape are cut into a thin substrate such as a metal sheet or waxed paper through which the colourant is applied; the other colours are masked out. In Japan stencils are still used to create the incredibly intricate designs that are printed onto kimonos.

Examples of positive and negative paper stencils and their corresponding printed results.

HAND SCREEN-PRINTING

A silk screen is made by stretching a fine, porous mesh over a frame. The design is then delineated by masking out areas of the design that will not be printed, leaving areas open for each colour, through which the ink is pushed using a rubber squeegee. The image that has been transferred onto the screen may also be laid out as a repeat.

The use of photochemical processes as a technique for exposing a template onto a silk screen that has been coated with a light-sensitive emulsion increased the range of effects that can be accurately reproduced. This technique involves copying the artwork onto transparent film (one per colour), so that each colour is isolated as a greyscale containing gradated tones from black to light grey, allowing one colourant to be reproduced as a series of shades. This transparency is then placed against the emulsion and the image transferred as the emulsion is hardened in the non-image areas by exposure to UV light. The un-hardened emulsion in the areas to be printed is then washed out, opening up the pores in the screen through which the ink will pass.

Most textile and fashion colleges provide students with studios equipped for silk-screen printing. The screen is moved systematically down the length of a piece of fabric to create a continuous design.

MECHANIZED FLATBED SILK-SCREEN PRINTING

The silk-screen printing process was first mechanized in 1954, when the flatbed process was introduced. Mechanized rollers feed the fabric under flat rectangular screens and the ink is applied using automated squeegees. More sophisticated flatbed printers are still used in print houses today, in the printing of luxury fabrics – the designs for which may contain up to 60 colours. Flatbed screen printing is much slower than rotary screen-printing (see below). In the Lake Como region of Italy, famous for the superiority of its print houses, many companies use traditional printing technologies alongside digital techniques to produce some of the world's most luxurious fabrics.

Mechanized flatbed screen printer.

ROTARY SCREEN-PRINTING

Rotary screen-printing was also developed in the mid 1950s in order to speed up production, and is currently the most widely-used method of textile printing, currently accounting for around 80 percent of printed textile production. Instead of a flat screen, this process uses a cylinder made from a very fine, reinforced metallic mesh. Initially the mesh is blocked, which entails coating the screen with a special emulsion and then burning out the areas to be printed using a computer-controlled laser. These cylindrical screens rotate as the cloth is moved under them at a high speed, and the ink is pushed through the mesh from the inside by a specially-designed squeegee. In this way, single colours are laid down successively as the cloth passes under each cylindrical screen to build up the full-colour image. The cost of rotary screen-printing is significantly less than flatbed silk-screen printing.

A cylindrical rotary screen that is used to print a single 'spot' colour in the mass production process.

PHOTOGRAPHIC FULL-COLOUR PRINTING

Four-colour printing is the most common method used by the reprographic industries in the printing of books and magazines as well as in the heat-transfer method of textile printing. Unlike traditional textile printing technology, where the image is built up using pre-mixed flat or 'spot' colours, the photographic or full-colour method of printing known as four-colour or process printing involves the separation of the original image into the four colours (CMYK) used in the subtractive colour model (see page 182). Additionally, in order to prepare the printing plates, a half-toning or screening process is also applied. This may be carried out digitally or by using photographic filters and results in a pattern of coloured dots. The spacing of these dots is varied, with some overlapping in order to create the illusion of thousands of colours.

Dot matrix image showing four-colour separation.

The print for this Paul Smith jacket has been separated using the four-colour process and printed onto paper then heat-transfer printed directly onto the fabric.

HEAT-TRANSFER PRINTING

While it was discovered in the late 1920s, the commercial development of transfer printing occurred during the 1960s and involves the printing or painting of transfer inks onto paper which will bond to certain fabrics upon heating. There are several methods of heat-transfer but the most commercially viable is sublimation printing. The sublimation process turns a solid into a gas and back into a solid again. The paper can be printed by any paper-printing method, and this increased the range of imagery that could be printed. It became possible to reproduce photographic images on textiles, though the process was mainly limited to synthetic fabrics.

As well as these industrial applications, transfer inks can be painted with an ink-like substance directly onto paper and then heat-transferred onto fabric, allowing a spontaneous approach to be taken.

Highly detailed sublimation printing of photographic imagery onto a polyester shirt. This 'Hobie' aloha shirt was typical in the 1970s.

COMMERCIAL VIABILITY OF TRADITIONAL VS DIGITAL PRINTING METHODS

Although digital printing is the fastest-growing method of textile printing, at the time of writing less than one percent of the world's textiles are digitally printed, with silk-screen printing still accounting for eighty percent of the global output of printed textiles. This is because rotary screen-printing technology is more financially viable for the mass-market sector of the industry.

SPEED

The industry standard for digital printers at the time of writing is to print up to 250 linear metres (273 yards) per hour, giving traditional methods the advantage, achieving up to 3000 linear metres (3280 yards) of fabric per hour. However, the newly-developed ISIS printer looks to be capable of rivalling rotary print production speeds. However, while the print time is fast with traditional methods, the lead time needed for a print to get into production is much slower. For example, it can take 8-12 weeks to get traditional textile prints into mass production, while digital production is almost instantaneous. This is because traditional printing plants require someone to colour separate the design, manage the repeat pattern, engrave screens, colour match and print a strike off (sample) for customer approval before proceeding to production. With digital printing the process only requires colour matching and printing off for customer approval, reducing the lead time significantly.

EXPENSE

Printing numerous colours has cost implications with rotary screen-printing (as a separate screen must be prepared for each colour), whereas with digital printing there is no difference whether you have three or unlimited colours in your design. The cost of dyes and inks can vary significantly with traditional methods, and a lot of research is being carried out in this area. Pigments have many advantages over other dyes: they are more lightfast and retain colour better after washing; they can be cheaper; can be printed on a broader range of fabrics; require less intervention in the fixation process.

VERSATILITY

A clear advantage of traditional methods over digital printing is the ability to complete more than one process, such as discharge printing, resist techniques, devoré, flocking, relief techniques and printing with metallic and pearlescent pigments. Research is being completed into these areas, but currently none are yet commercially available for use in digital printing.

DIGITAL TEXTILE PRINT TECHNOLOGY

'Digital printing' is a generic term used to describe all methods of printing where a digitized image is transferred onto the substrate. Currently there are two different types of digital print technology. The first of these, electrostatic (also known as laser printing), only works with paper and is the technology used in colour copying machines and some office printers. The second method, known as inkjet printing, can be divided into two categories: continuous flow and drop on demand (DOD). In turn, DOD technology has two subcategories: thermal and piezo electric. Piezo electric DOD inkjet technology is currently the primary method for the digital printing of textiles and is used in printers such as the Mimaki.

Inkjet printing may be defined as a process by which the desired pattern is built up by projecting tiny drops of 'ink' of different colours, in predetermined micro-arrays (pixels), onto the substrate surface. The ink is projected onto the surface as a controlled series of drops by using electromagnetic fields to guide electrically-charged ink-streams onto the fabric. ('Ink' is the generic term primarily used in conjunction with digital printing and refers to both dyes and pigments.)

The mechanism that is responsible for this is the print head, which is an electromechanical device that contains ink, a feed system, a drop-formation mechanism, nozzles and usually the ink-supply in tanks or cartridges. The print head is moved across the fabric to deposit drops of ink in the correct positions.

THE ADAPTATION OF DIGITAL PRINTING TECHNOLOGY FOR TEXTILES

Technology for the digital printing of textiles developed out of technology initially devised for printing on paper; large-format textile printers are essentially wider versions of smaller desktop printers that have been adapted to handle wide rolls of substrate instead of small sheets of paper. Digital printing is now used for printing onto a wide range of materials, including natural fibre-based substrates such as cotton, silk and wool cloth as well as polyester-based fabrics, linoleum and Formica.

There are two methods used for the inkjet printing of textiles: indirect inkjet heat-transfer printing and direct inkjet printing, both of which are examined on the following pages.

The digital printing process for textiles differs from that for paper because of the fixation process necessary to make the fabric washable and colourfast. This means that the printing process is less direct and involves more steps due to the chemical reaction that must take place between the fabric, the dyes or pigments, and the fixing agents.

Basic mechanics of the print head used in piezo electric DOD inkjet technology.

- nozzle
- charging system
- deflector
- gutter
- droplets
- ink supply
- substrate

Short-run textile printers such as the Mimaki TX2 (below) became available for general use in 1998 and are widely used in large print houses as well as smaller studios. Mass-production printers such as the Robustelli Mona-Lisa (above) were first introduced in 2003.

INDIRECT INKJET/ HEAT-TRANFER PRINTING

As mentioned earlier in this chapter, heat-transfer printing enabled images that could be printed onto paper by any traditional graphic printing method to be transferred onto fabric. This process was commercially exploited in the 1960s and 70s, but, because the process could only work effectively with synthetic fabrics, its application was limited. The development of large-scale digital printers enabled the production of transfer papers, and the range of fabrics a print could be bonded to has expanded dramatically.

Another application of this process is in the growing arena of individual novelty products, where clients' photographs are printed onto bags, T-shirts and even soft furnishings. This can be achieved by photocopying an image or printing it on your home inkjet printer onto specially-finished papers.

Large-scale or mass-production heat-transfer printing is accomplished by first printing an image onto paper using a wide-format inkjet printer, and then transferring it onto fabric through the use of a heated roller machine (or calender). Heat transfer via inkjet-printed disperse dyes onto transfer paper is the primary method used in the printing of swimwear and sportswear today.

On a smaller scale in the home or studio, it is possible to buy heat-transfer paper which may be printed with a desktop inkjet printer; the image is then transferred onto cloth with an iron or a small heat-press. DIY photographic T-shirt printing works by using the heat from an iron to adhere a digitally-printed plastic layer onto the cotton of the shirt. This plastic layer is necessary because dye sublimation does not work with natural fibres.

This dynamic cushion by Jemima Gregson was sublimation printed onto faux suede.

'Owl' by Petra Boase. This children's T-shirt was digitally designed and printed on high-quality transfer paper and applied via heat-press.

Photini Anastasi achieves soft and subtle photographic effects by sublimation printing onto polyester chiffon.

DIRECT INKJET PRINTING PROCESS

The following sequence demonstrates the process of inkjet textile printing from start to finish, and shows how a detailed and colourful photographic design can be printed onto fabric.

1 The roll of fabric is loaded onto the back of the printer. The fabric is then fed through to the front by passing it under a series of small rollers that run along the width of the printer, ensuring that the fabric will be fed smoothly as the print head runs across it.

3 The height of the print head is then adjusted according to the thickness of the substrate.

5 The design is opened into the RIP or print-driver software and parameters such as the number of repeats to be tiled out and the length of the print run are entered. The print-driver software is also used to set variables such as print speed, number of passes for the print head and how much ink will be laid down.

2 The fabric is attached to a motorized roller system that automatically winds the fabric forward under the moving print heads once the printer is in action. Careful attention must be paid to ensure that the tension of the length of fabric is correct and that the fabric is straight. In some cases the fabric is interleaved with tissue paper to blot any excess ink during the print run. A bar that runs across the width is clamped down to stop the fabric from crumpling as it passes under the rollers.

4 A series of printer tests are carried out, including a 'media compensation' and a nozzle check. The media compensation setting adjusts the speed of the printer according to how much stretch the fabric has and the nozzle test indicates whether all eight print heads are firing correctly.

6 The design file is then sent to the printer via the RIP to begin printing. Before proceeding to the final length, samples are printed, steamed and washed to check colour and image quality. Some fabrics require that the ink needs to be left to dry before proceeding to the next step.

7 There are several ways of preparing cloth for steaming. Muslin, steaming paper or a fine plastic mesh may be used as a barrier to stop the ink from bleeding onto itself during steaming. In all cases, one of these porous materials is interleaved with the print, forming a protective layer through which the steam can pass

8 The fabric is loaded into a steamer, to be steamed for a specific time to fix the colour. If the design has been printed using pigments or disperse dyes, these colourants are fixed via heat rather than steam in a baking oven.

9 The fabric is washed to remove coating and excess colourant, and ironed. It is very important not to overload the washing machine as the image may bleed onto itself.

INKJET PRINTING TIPS

In ensuring the success of any inkjet printing it is important to remember the following:

Never underestimate the importance of sampling.

Remember that colours will brighten after printing (unless pigments have been used), and that the 'hand' of the cloth will soften – in other words, if you feel that a fabric you are considering is too stiff, remember that once the coating has washed out and it has been ironed this will change.

If you print a 'sketch' of an initial idea, then in proceeding to a final print it is crucial that no aspects of the final file originating from the sample have changed.

Consider setting aside a roll with enough fabric for the final print as a new roll of the same fabric may produce slightly different results.

Protect unprinted fabrics from light.

Keep the printer scrupulously clean.

Don't allow any water near unsteamed fabric.

Keep the steamer in a separate, well-ventilated room.

Garment made from the finished fabric featuring a floral print designed by Daisy Butler and printed on the Mimaki TX2.

CHEMISTRY AND FIXATION OF COLOURANTS

In order for cloth to retain its colour for a reasonable period of time after repeated washing and exposure to sunlight, a chemical reaction must first take place between the fabric, the dye or pigment, and, in some cases, the fixation agent – a chemical that attaches to receptor sites on the surface of the fibres and makes a chemical bridge between the dyestuff and the fibre. This process is achieved by either steaming or heating the cloth after it has been printed.

PRE-TREATING FABRIC

Unlike traditional methods of printing, where the fixing agent is mixed into the dye or pigment, in digital textile printing the fixation agent is applied as a special coating onto the fabric before printing. This coating is also designed to ensure that when the droplets of ink hit the surface of the cloth they do not spread, so that the details of a design are maintained and are not blurred. This coating is basically comprised of an alginate thickener for reactive dyes and carbohydrate-based or synthetic thickener for acid or disperse dyes. The fixing agent for reactive dyes is alkaline soda ash, whereas a weak acid is used for acid dye. There is no need for a fixative in the case of disperse dyes.

It is possible to experiment with the inkjet printing of certain fabrics by silk screening the coating mixture onto the fabric yourself. However, in the printing of longer lengths it is more practical and will yield better results if you buy rolls of fabric that have been pre-coated by a specialist company. The chemicals in the coating are specific to the dye that will be used, so it is important to check.

In order to achieve consistent colour and detail it is crucial that the coating has been applied evenly. If there is a significant variation either in the chemistry or the amount of coating that has been applied to two different rolls of the same type of fabric, it is probable that the printed colours will not match. In some cases, if the chemical formula for the coating is not correct then the ink may bleed or not dry properly. The coating may stiffen and in some cases will dull the sheen of certain cloths temporarily. Once it has been washed and steamed, however, it will regain its original sheen, softness and drape.

TYPES OF INKJET COLOURANT

There are two categories of colourant used: dyes and pigments. The chemistry of dyes and pigments used in inkjet printing of textiles is based on that used in the traditional dyeing or silk screening of fabrics, with the essential difference that only synthetic dyes and pigments may be used. The viscosity of pigments that have been designed for use in an inkjet textile printer has also been modified so that the print heads do not become blocked. Technological advances in digital printing have also led to improvements in the way that pigment-based inks adhere to the surface of the fabric.

DYES Specific dyes must be used for different types of fabric. There are three categories of materials used in the making of textiles. These are plant (cellulose), animal (protein) and synthetic-based fibres. Acid dyes work only with protein-based materials and nylon, while reactive dyes may be used with both plant-based and animal-based materials. Disperse dyes have been developed for the colouration of synthetic polymer-based materials. The colours that may be achieved vary according to the type of dye used. Acid dyes produce colours that are brighter than those created by reactive dyes. It is not possible, for example, to attain a 'neon' green by using a reactive dye. However, disperse dyes also result in very bright colours.

PIGMENTS In contrast to dyes, pigments may be used more universally. Unlike dyes, they do not directly associate with the textile fibres but are fixed to the surface of the cloth with a 'binding agent'. Pigments are bonded to the surface of the fabric by heat. The colours that result from printing with pigments are duller than those achieved with dyes.

As pigments sit on the surface of the cloth, fabrics such as silk satin will lose some of their shine after printing and will also become slightly stiffer than they would if printed with dye. Despite these disadvantages pigments are widely used in textile printing as they may be used on all types of fabric and are also intrinsically more colourfast than dyes. They are often less expensive, too. The most significant advantage of using pigments in an inkjet printer is that the fabric does not require pre-treatment or coating.

DELIVERY OF INK INTO THE PRINTER

There are two methods of delivering dyes or pigments into a printer. Suppliers of inkjet printing materials sell cartridges that are similar to those used in a desktop photographic printer; however cartridges designed for use in a large-format textile printer contain a larger quantity of ink. 'Bulk-feed' systems have also been developed where a separate device is connected to the printer and feeds ink into it from a bottle. Such bulk-feed systems are more economical, as the cost of textile ink cartridges can be prohibitive. It is also possible to use special cartridges designed to be refilled with ink from a bottle using a syringe. This method will also prove more economical than using disposable cartridges. When using either a bulk-feed system or cartridges it is very important to prevent air bubbles from entering the ink-feed lines as these cause the print heads to become blocked.

THE FIXATION PROCESS

DYES After the fabric has been printed it is rolled up and sandwiched between a layer of special paper, plastic mesh or hessian cloth, so that ink will not transfer from one side of the cloth to the other. This also facilitates the transfer of steam to the interior of the roll. There are several types of steamers used in the dye-fixation process. Small studios use a simple device consisting of an upright metal cylinder with a removable lid, in which water is heated to boiling point by an electrical element. These steamers are designed so that the fabric rests on a platform at the base of the steamer and the roll is held vertically by a device at the top, ensuring that it does not come in contact either with the water or the condensation that may form on the inside of the cylinder itself.

If water does comes into contact with the roll it will cause the ink to bleed, resulting in a blurred image or one that – in severe cases – disappears entirely. Steaming time varies according to the type of steamer as well as the type of dye. If conditions vary within the steamer, or if the vapour is not evenly distributed, then colours will not be consistent. These upright steamers are only capable of steaming around 10 metres (11 yards) of fabric. It is also possible to fix fabric by hanging it in a steam chamber or cabinet.

In a factory setting, industrial-scale steamers are used for mass-production. Mid-range equipment capable of accommodating up to 50 metres (54 yards) of fabric is also available, and priced at an affordable level for smaller studios. These devices are more sophisticated than the small steamer described above, making it easier to control temperature and pressure. Timing can be automated, as can the release of steam at the end of the cycle. Steam-time is also shorter in an industrial steamer.

It is very important that all steamers are properly ventilated and that, upon release, the steam produced is filtered by an extraction device in order to remove any toxic fumes. Technicians should also wear gas masks.

PIGMENTS Fabrics that have been printed with pigments are fixed by baking them in a special oven or heat-press.

DISPERSE DYES These may be digitally printed directly onto the substrate and then fixed by heating. Alternatively, in the inkjet transfer process, the image may be printed onto special paper and then fixed and transferred simultaneously onto the fabric by passing the substrate through heated rollers or under a heat-press. Synthetic fabrics and polyester-coated Formica and ceramics are all fixed in this way.

WASHING

After fixation, the fabric is washed to remove excess dye. Each batch of a longer run must be washed by machine under exactly the same conditions to maintain consistency. The washing machine should not be overloaded because if the cloth is packed too tightly it may become stained. Domestic washing machines usually accommodate around 10 metres (11 yards) of fabric. An industrial washing machine should be used for lengths above this amount. Fabrics should be washed until the water runs as clear of dye as is possible. Stickiness resulting from any residue of the coating may be removed by further washing. Temperature settings are the same as for non digitally printed fabrics. Once washed, the fabric should not be left crumpled as staining may occur.

Here, the same design has been printed on a number of different substrates – silk jersey, silk chiffon and silk satin (left to right) – to test how colour and finish differ.

	Acid dye (Steam)	Reactive dye (Steam)	Disperse dye (Heat)	Pigments (Heat)
Silk	o	o		o
Wool	o	o		o
Linen		o		o
Cotton		o		o
Nylon	o			o
Polyester			o	o
Rayon		o		o

This chart shows the types of colourant, and their corresponding fixation processes, that can be used for different substrates.

ADVANTAGES OF DIGITAL PRINTING

Digital printing, as we outlined in the early section, can have many advantages over traditional printing methods, in speed and efficiency and costs at smaller manufacturing numbers. However, at present it cannot compete with costs at large meterage. With research being carried out into this area it will perhaps be able to compete more directly in time.

These cost and efficiency savings only demonstrate one half of the story: where inkjet printing makes a difference is in lessened environmental impact, and design advantages. From a design perspective, the ability to print full-colour, detailed designs using any scale, repeat or non-repeating elements and engineered prints opens up a wealth of creative possibilities.

REDUCED ENVIRONMENTAL IMPACT

Inkjet printing has more environmental advantages than conventional printing methods, and a more sustainable future will be possible if this production method is adopted over others. This is primarily due to there being less wastage of dye, as the ink is printed on demand, and fabric can be printed as all-over fabric or to specific pattern placements, thereby reducing fabric wastage. Inkjet printing is reported to use 30 percent less water and 45 percent less electricity than conventional printing methods. These savings mean that the process has less impact on the environment than traditional print processes.

RAPID TURNAROUND

Once a design file has been finalized, the technical set-up time for an inkjet printer is minimal. In comparison to most traditional print methods – which typically involve several preparatory steps before printing can begin – digital printing is direct, and turnaround time for short runs is fast. A Mimaki TX2 printer, for example, can produce between 3 and 28 linear metres (3½ and 30½ yards) per hour, depending on image quality, and uses 16 Epson-type print-heads that may accommodate eight colours. As the name implies,

short-run printers are capable of producing a smaller quantity of printed goods to be used as prototypes, one-offs or limited edition products. However, such printers may also be set up as multiple installations in digital print production facilities in order to print larger volumes.

Printers capable of mass-production were first released in 2003 and can typically print around 250 linear metres (273 yards) per hour. The best known manufacturers are Dupont (Artistry), Reggiani (DReAM), Robustelli (Mona-Lisa), Mimaki (TX2). However, Osiris have produced the first full production machine capable of printing 1800 metres (1968 yards) an hour – around 30 metres (33 yards) a minute – with their ISIS printer, creating a new industry standard.

The immediacy and minimal set-up time for digital printing also means that fashion and textile houses no longer need to warehouse additional fabric stock in advance of manufacturing the final goods, resulting in less wastage. Print-runs can be set up on demand to match orders from retailers as they come in.

This rapid turnaround time is also advantageous for the designer. For most artists and designers the successful realization of an idea usually involves a process of trial, re-evaluation and adaptation. Digital printing is literally one step behind the designer's imagination and facilitates the flow of ideas in design development.

UNLIMITED COLOUR AND DETAIL

There's virtually no limit to the type of image that may be reproduced using digital inkjet fabric printing technology as it is based on the CMYK or process-colour method for photographic printing. Half-toning of primary CMYK colours means that millions of colours are perceived by the viewer, limited only by the colour gamut of the dye in relation to the substrate. Extremely bright colours may be achieved using acid dyes, but neon colours are

The Dutch Company OSIRIS has recently developed the ISIS printer, which is set to rival the speeds of rotary screen-printing as it is capable of printing 30 linear metres (33 yards) per minute. The ISIS uses continuous-flow inkjet technology as well as an unusual principle whereby a fixed row of print heads span the width of the printer.

not yet attainable with the inks currently available. Due to the photographic foundation of this technology, most of the subtleties and nuances of the original image may now be translated in detail onto fabric.

INCREASED SCALE

One of the first reactions from designers upon the introduction of digital print for textiles was excitement at the fact that repeat (of the design unit or croquis) was no longer necessary, as it was suddenly possible to print mural-sized images. Digital printing technology means that the only limit to the size of a design is the software's capacity to handle large files.

A bigger canvas and the ability to lay out extended placement prints is changing the way designers approach print, although there will always be aesthetic reasons for continuing to use repeated patterns. Facilitated by the possibility of developing software programming for longer design lengths, research has begun into the generation and printing of randomized, continuously changing structures such as those found in biological growth patterns.

ENGINEERING DESIGNS

In general, the mass market utilizes print to 'fill' in the garment outlines rather than to interact with the garment and body. Print is placed on top of garment shapes rather than being developed in unison. This often creates a clumsy and inappropriate use of print. Inkjet printing engenders a stronger relationship between the product and image. By printing the image to exact specification of a garment or product, print designers can more fully engage with the relationship between form and image.

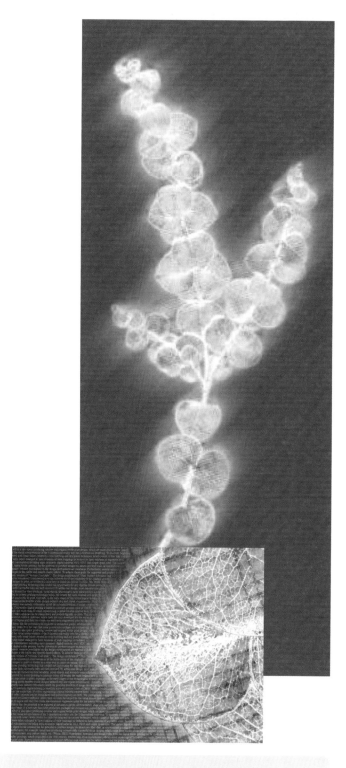

'Branch', by Hitoshi Ujiie (2005), makes use of two of the most significant advantages that digital design and printing has over traditional methods: the piece is 3.5 metres (nearly 4 yards) high and, when viewed more closely, reveals an extraordinarily high level of detail.

DISADVANTAGES OF DIGITAL INKJET PRINTING

The most prohibitive factor in the adoption of digital inkjet technology is that it is still much more expensive than screen-printing and heat-transfer methods. While the costs are coming down, it will take a substantial period of development and integration to begin to compete with rotary printing. Commercially, many digital printers are currently only used for sampling and to create prototypes that will eventually be produced using traditional methods. At the time of writing, less than one percent of the world's textiles are printed digitally.

In design terms, the advantages of digital fabric printing far outweigh those of traditional methods, but digital printing is not yet capable of some of the decorative effects that are possible with silk screening, such as devoré and flocking. It is also not yet capable of printing metallic inks onto fabric. Research is currently underway into the development of these techniques.

DIGITAL TEXTILE DESIGN AND PRINTING SOFTWARE

Behind digital printing is a range of software that is used in the design process and also in the preparation of the design for print. This only came within the remit of textile designers once the technology for the digital printing of textiles became viable in 1998. The off-the-shelf package Adobe Illustrator was first released in 1987 as a font-development program for graphic designers, and Adobe Photoshop followed in 1990. Although textile designers would have been able to use these tools, they were still largely the domain of photographers and graphic designers, as images created through their use could only be realized on paper. Therefore the advertising, publishing and photographic industries led the way in the development of digital-imaging software and a true digital style for textiles would only emerge ten years later.

Using a specialist CAD system to set up a design to print. On the right is a light box that is used to match colours within a calibrated system.

USING SPECIALIST CAD SYSTEMS

As well as off-the-shelf imaging software, there is a range of specialist CAD systems available to the printed textile industry. These programs are generally designed to be used by companies who will mass-produce their products, as in most cases, although they are capable of taking in images that contain millions of colours, ultimately their purpose is to systematically reduce these colours down to the number of screens that will be used to engrave screens for rotary printing (a process known as colour separation). Unlike Photoshop, which was designed primarily for the reprographic industries, specialist CAD programs contain tools that aid in the design-creation aspects that are unique to surface design, including the creation of colourways, the touching-up of a design ready for the engraver and automatic live time-repeat function. Many also include sophisticated colour-management systems. Although it is possible to carry out such operations using off-the-shelf software, specialist CAD programs streamline

the process of preparing an image for print. Adobe Photoshop and Illustrator do, however, provide excellent tools for designers who intend to print shorter runs digitally and wish to retain the photographic quality of an image.

COLOUR SEPARATION

Within the context of the textile industry, colour separation, also known as colour reduction, is a process that reduces the number of colours in an image down to a finite number of flat or 'spot' colours, usually shown as black and white shapes that represent the set of motifs that contain each colour (typically less than ten colours at the lower end of the market and many more for luxury goods). Tonal separations may also be created as greyscales in order to simulate images that contain thousands of colours, though in fact only a limited number of colours are used in the printing process.

These images show the four colour separations that have been creating using CAD in order to engrave the four screens required to print this flat colour design using traditional methods. Colour samples may be printed digitally to replicate final production.

This is an example of a design containing tonal effects. The eight colour tonal separations have been created by reducing the millions of colours found in the original scan down to eight screens ready for rotary screen printing.

Colour separation serves two purposes. The first is to prepare an image for rotary screen-printing; each separation is used to create one screen that will be printed in sequence in the mill. The second is that it makes colour-matching and the creation of colourways much easier. If a design is to be printed digitally then colour separation will also mean that it will be easier to 'plug in' matching colours across a range of coordinating designs such as borders or matching all-over prints.

Colour separation can be a highly-skilled art, requiring much practice in an industry setting. Companies such as Hermès and Colefax and Fowler rely on separation artists who are masters of their craft. Most of the artwork used by high-end home-furnishing companies such as Sanderson's in the UK is painted by hand, and, although the final design may look deceptively simple, the scan of the original contains thousands of colours and a series of steps must be carried out before the screens can be engraved.

COLOURWAYS AND COLOUR-PALETTE DATABASES

A colourway is a term used in the textile industry to describe versions of the same design that have been coloured differently. Usually, although the colours in each colourway will be different, they follow a set order from light to dark to help organize them for the printing process. Most specialist CAD textile systems also provide colour-palette databases than can be organized by collection or season in order to facilitate the transfer of a set of colours automatically into an entire collection.

LIVE TIME-REPEAT

Automatic live time-repeat functions work by creating almost instantaneous repeats, including half-drops, and can be extremely useful when preparing a print. As many repeat units as are desired may be viewed or 'tiled' across large widths, and when a motif is moved or manipulated all its copies in the repeat grid change at once. Automatic repeat systems may be more sophisticated in a specialist system; however, add-on software is available at prices aimed at individual designers.

Alternative colourways for a design that are based on the same colour-separation template.

WORKING WITH COLOUR

Our perception of colour is subjective and this, in part, makes our interpretation and translation of colour from one technology to another difficult. Another factor in this difficulty is the difference between additive and subtractive colour. Subtractive colours are those that are made from a combination of primaries cyan, magenta and yellow: these colours absorb light and are the colours we see in printed inks and dyes. In theory, mixing them all together creates black. The colours that we see on a monitor are the result of emitted light and are made by mixing the primary colours red, green and blue: these are described as the additive model. In the additive model, mixing all three RGB primaries results in white. Digital cameras, scanners and monitors all use this additive RGB model as a basis for displaying or interpreting colour, and prints on paper or textiles use the subtractive model.

THE SCREEN TO PRINT DILEMMA

In digital printing, achieving the colours we desire may be solved in two ways; either by carrying out manual adjustments and colour tests or by incorporating separate colour-management software into the set up of a digital-print studio.

Newcomers to digital textile printing may encounter some difficulties in areas that relate to colour and the workflow that is necessary to obtain the desired results. Many of the issues that arise around colour and digital printing are often based on the mistaken assumption that the colours viewed on screen will automatically match those in the final print. This is not the case. When finalizing colours for a design that is to be digitally printed it is crucial to understand that what we see on screen is relative and it should not be taken for granted that the colours we have chosen will be reproduced exactly unless colour-management software has been used.

There are two reasons for this: firstly, although all monitors and display devices use RGB technology, each individual type of device will display the same colour differently unless they have been calibrated. Again, unless calibrated, printers of the same kind also have different 'fingerprints' and it is likely they will display the same design differently. Additionally, it is the translation of RGB data into the CYMK data necessary to control a printer that will cause a discrepancy between displayed and printed colours.

(Left) RGB additive colour model of emitted light used to generate the colours displayed by monitors. (Right) CMYK subtractive colour model of absorbed light.

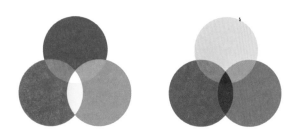

LINKING TO THE PRINTER, PRINT DRIVERS AND RIP SOFTWARE

Most set-ups for desk-top printing incorporate a program known as a print driver or Raster Image Processor – RIP – that is either supplied by the software company such as Photoshop or by a printer vendor such as Epson. However, drivers for large-format printers, like the Mimaki, are not built-in and so it is necessary to invest in a specialist print driver as the printer may not be operated without it. In digital textile printing the role that the driver plays in controlling print quality and the smooth running of a studio or 'factory' can not be underestimated, and it is vital when setting up a new studio to research and choose the appropriate software carefully.

A RIP is software that rasterizes, or converts, the RGB data from the matrix of pixels (bitmap) in a displayed image into the CMYK information that will 'drive' the printer. This software also dictates variables such as print speed and resolution as well as the number of print-head passes and the quantity of ink that will be laid down thus affecting colour. If colour management has been incorporated then it is through the print driver that a technician will set the profiles described earlier in order to accommodate each type of fabric. Importantly, textile RIPs will also tile-out a design unit as a repeat as well as automatically incorporating half-drops. Such drivers are also designed specifically to accommodate very large designs as well as extremely long-run print lengths necessary for mass production.

SPECIALIST COLOUR-MANAGEMENT SYSTEMS

A range of specialist colour-management technology has been developed for the photographic and reprographic businesses as well as for other industries where colour accuracy is vital. The purpose of these systems is to streamline and facilitate the process of handling colour as it is translated from one device to another through to the final production. A highly sophisticated textile system is, for example, able to send the colour data necessary for dye formulation directly to a mill.

Most colour-management systems work by mediating between and coordinating the various input and output devices used in a given workflow environment and managing the way that colour data is used and transferred between them. Central to colour management is a process known as calibration that works as a loop and involves a feedback mechanism that begins by printing a set of files using the primary CMYK inks. These colours are analyzed by the technician in order to determine the best printer settings for each individual fabric type – such as how much ink a particular fabric may absorb before the colour will bleed. These samples are then read in using a spectrophotometer (an instrument for measuring spectral transmittance or reflectance), and the data is used to generate a series of files – known as printer profiles – that will individualize print controls for each fabric type. Essentially, at this stage, the basic printer controls are being fine-tuned before a greater range of colours are analyzed.

Within a set-up that has been calibrated, multiple printers, as well as monitors, may be included within a closed system. These profiles are then applied to a comprehensive set of colour samples that have been generated systematically by the software in order to print, comparing them with the corresponding colours from the same file as they appear on the display. A spectrophotometer is again used to read in each colour chip in the printed 'target' sample for each fabric type once the colorant has been fixed and washed. Similarly, a series of colour targets are also measured on screen by placing a spectrophotometer against the monitor. This data is then processed by the software and used to fine tune the colours as displayed using RGB data in order to match those found in the final print. The spectral difference between the displayed and printed colours is compiled by the software in order to create profiles for each monitor and fabric type.

The advantage of this process is that, when a particular profile is applied to a displayed image, the designer will be able to judge more accurately what the final colour results will be and see how they would change if a different dye or pigment were to be used in printing. If it is not possible to obtain, for example, a very bright red using pigments or a certain fabric type then some programs will show the closest match within the colour space. Currently, however, there are certain colours that may be displayed on screen that are not possible to reproduce under any circumstances due to the limitations of the dyes and colourants used in textile printing. An achievable colour is described as being 'in gamut', whereas any colour that may not be displayed or printed is described as being 'out of gamut' (see right).

Colours taken from paper or fabric swatches may also be input into a design by using a spectrophotometer to measure them and so automatically generating a match once printed. It is important to take into consideration when using fabric or paper colour samples for matching, that the same colour will appear to be different depending on whether it is applied to a glossy, matt or transparent substrate. Similarly, the colours in your print will appear to change if viewed under different conditions such as day or fluorescent light. A specialist piece of equipment known as a light box will facilitate this.

Tests carried our during printer calibration in order to implement ink settings such as the quantity of ink to be laid down for each fabric type. The above image shows that too much ink has been laid down, causing the dye to bleed.

A set of achievable colours within a 3D model of a specific colour space. Unachievable colours are 'out of gamut'.

Colour matching yarn and fabric swatches.

Using a spectrophotometer to read in a colour target in order to generate a specific profile containing individual printer settings.

REVITALIZING THE TEXTILE INDUSTRY

Digital print is revitalizing the textile industry, not only in terms of design, but also production. Many established print companies in Italy and Japan are seeking to maintain their links with their couture clients – who are starting to explore digital design – by introducing digital print technology alongside traditional methods. Companies in China are also making a considerable investment in the new technology, while digital-print bureaus are emerging in countries that have largely lost their fabric production to Asia. The relatively low cost of the equipment is also encouraging designers to set up their own print studios.

DIGITAL PRINT HOUSES

Many of the print-houses in Como, Italy – such as Mantero and Ratti, who produce some of the world's most luxurious fabrics, and who are considered by many designers to be a centre of excellence for printed textiles – have been using the latest technology alongside traditional methods ever since the first digital textile printers became available. The philosophy behind companies such as Ratti is that the quality of the prints they produce is far more important than quantity or cost. Investing in state-of-the-art technology is crucial to maintaining the competitive edge to the extent that some Como printers do not simply buy this equipment but work hand-in-hand with its developers to constantly improve the technology. Suffice to say, Como textile printing is considered an art.

In Japan the company Seiren was also a pioneer of inkjet textile printing and began testing the viability of this technology as long ago as the early 1980s. By 1991, they had introduced inkjet printing alongside traditional methods; one of their primary markets being the market for custom car interiors. Companies in China such as Huang Wha have also begun to make considerable investments in inkjet textile-printing plants.

Using CAD to set up an image to print at the Ratti plant.

The design studio, where traditional techniques such as hand painting are used alongside digital tools.

The 4,600-square-metre (50,000-square-foot) Ratti print facility, situated on a plateau above Como in Italy.

Large-scale digital printing in action.

DIGITAL-PRINT BUREAUS

As the cost of a large-format inkjet printer is considerably less than the equipment necessary to set up a rotary screen-printing plant, many small digital-print bureaus are emerging, specializing in the printing of textiles. Bureau printing services provide an invaluable resource for students, independent designers and larger commercial companies alike. Some operate out of an artist's loft, while others are set up like small factories with multiple printers, catering to a growing demand for innovative and unusual products. These small businesses will support the growing demand for designer- and customized goods.

Small bureaus allow designers to produce prototype short runs of fabric and have access to face-to-face consultation. Sampling printed cloth in the traditional way can be extremely expensive and time consuming, and this can inhibit designers who want to see printed results fast. Using a bureau, it is possible to see and approve fabric at different stages in the sampling process and try out new ideas during the development process. Dan Locastro of First2Print, a digital bureau in New York, observes that 'we can print in a fraction of the time it would take for a fabric manufacturer to get samples ready for showrooms, sales development and photoshoots'.

Students are now using digital-print bureaus to implement their designs. Learning to out-source in this way helps to smooth the transition from education to operating as an independent business in terms of gaining experience in budgeting, communication and management, but it is important that students also maintain a hands-on approach to the digital printing process.

USING A BUREAU

Different digital bureaus use different hardware and software, so it is not really possible to give hard and fast rules as to preparation of files, etc., but Cameron Gilmartin, a London-based digital-print bureau, recommend following these basic rules of thumb:

Always build in time for sampling. It cannot be stressed enough what an essential part of the process this is.

Check shrinkage of the fabric you are printing onto: some fabrics shrink more than others and shrinkage will occur after printing so it's best to print a larger quantity initially.

Make sure your document is cropped to exactly the size you want, especially repeat units, as the printer will treat any white space as part of the design. If you are printing panels and want to include white space, include crop marks.

Remember that colour matching can be time consuming and therefore expensive, as samples may have to be steamed and washed each time in order to properly check colour.

These images detail the print process at New-York-based digital-print bureau, First2Print.
Left to right, top to bottom: Printer set-up within the design studio; loading the printer; printing in progress; checking and approving the final print.

THE FUTURE OF DIGITAL TEXTILE PRINTING

The technology behind digital printing is advancing rapidly and research is taking place into many potential avenues for its use in textile design and print. Smart colourants, such as thermochromic inks that change colour according to the temperature, are currently printed by silk screen but will undoubtedly be adapted for digital printing. Research is also currently underway into the inkjet printing of images onto flexible screens, using display technologies such as Organic Light-Emitting Polymers (OLEPs). It is likely that this will result in fabrics onto which changeable or moving images may be downloaded. As artists such as Maggie Orth (renowned for her work with interactive textiles) collaborate with scientists, the potential outcomes are beyond our imagination.

LED elements are being embedded into a variety of products. Hussein Chalayan used this technology to create a dress for his A/W 07/08 collection (right). Although LEDs are not digitally printed when applied to a garment, they provide a glimpse of what is to come.

Research is also underway into the digital printing of metallic inks – possible on other substrates, though currently not viable on cloth. Once developed, this will enable electric circuits that could double as decorative elements to be printed onto the surface of a garment.

The proportion of digital printing is clearly set to increase in the next decade as we see faster printers with a wider range of print possibilities develop. The range of inks and types of processes that may be possible could lead to new and exciting possibilities through digital mark-making qualities such as relief, burn out, density and depth of mark. This will require the development of inks and dyes that lie on top of, burn into or distort the fabric, and also fabric preparations to create effects such as resists and finishes using chemicals to distort or reveal layers of the textile.

Finally, the military, medical and cosmetic industries are also funding research into the micro-encapsulation of nanoparticles into ink, which could lead to the digital printing of antimicrobial agents on fabrics, including insect repellents, vitamins, skin conditioners and fragrances. As these technologies – and the means of applying them to substrates through digital design and print – advance, we can only speculate as to the exciting future of textile design.

Companies such as the Universal Display Corporation have been carrying out research into the development of flexible screen technology, which will enable moving images to be displayed onto flexible substrates. Here is a visualization of one such display that makes use of organic light-emitting polymer technology.

Hussein Chalayan (above) and Lumalive by Philips (below) provide a glimpse of what the future may hold in the integration of LED technology into their designs.

GLOSSARY

A

Alginate A substance extracted from seaweed that is used as a thickening agent.

Avatar A virtual depiction of a human figure, usually animated.

B

Batik A resist-based dyeing technique where wax is applied to a fabric in order to delineate the design by creating a mask before dyeing. (See also Shibori.)

Bespoke A one-of-a-kind customized product; made to order.

Body scanner A device that is used to capture measurements digitally in order to create a highly accurate 3D model of an individual's body.

C

CIE (Commission Internationale de l'Eclairage) This international commission on illumination, was established to create objective standards for defining and communicating colour.

CMYK Subtractive colour model consisting of cyan, magenta, yellow and key (black). In digital printing, these four basic ink colours are combined in a matrice of dots to create all the other colours that will be printed.

Colour Calibration The management and adjustment of colour data within a closed workflow environment for both input and output devices.

Colour Gamut A complete subset of colours that can be accurately represented for a given device, such as a monitor or printer. Different devices have different gamuts.

Colour Management A software system that controls the conversion of colour data for both input and output devices. The goal of a printed-textile colour management system is to aid the colour matching process as data is converted from emitted RGB into printable CMYK values.

Colour Profile Data characterizing the colour output of an individual device.

Colour Separation (also known as colour reduction) A process where the millions of colours found in a photographic or scanned image are systematically reduced down to a finite number of flat colours in order to prepare the design for printing or engraving, or to aid in the creation of colourways.

Colour Space A three-dimensional graphic model illustrating a set of colours in which the perceptual difference between colours is represented by points within the colour space.

Colourways A term used to describe versions of the same design that are composed of different colour palettes.

Continuous Flow Inkjet Technology (CIJ) One of the two types of inkjet printing technology; in this process a high-pressure pump directs liquid ink from a reservoir through a microscopic nozzle, thus creating a continuous stream of ink. (See also DOD.)

Coordinated Prints A group of print designs based on the same concept and colour palette, for use in conjunction with each other.

Croquis Term used to describe the original artwork of the design unit intended for a printed textile, before it is put into repeat.

D

Découpage A technique of decorating the surface of objects such as furniture or boxes by gluing paper cut outs and illustrations from magazines; this is then sealed with varnish to make a durable surface.

Delta e The unit used to quantify the difference between two colours within the CIE colour space.

Devoré (also known as burn-out) A method of printing onto fabric with more than one fibre type. The areas of the design are printed with a chemical that burns out one of the fabric's fibre types to leave a translucent area.

Digital Textile Printing A general term that includes all forms of digital printing such as laser and inkjet technology.

Discharge Printing A method of printing using chlorine or other chemicals to remove areas of previously applied colour and replace them with another colour.

DOD (Drop on Demand) One of the two types of inkjet printing technology and the most commonly used in digital textile printing; the primary DOD method used to print on textiles is known as piezo electric. (See also Continuous Flow Ink Technology.)

Dot Matrix In the case of inkjet printing, this is a two-dimensional pattern of CMYK dots that combine to generate the printed image.

dpi (dots per inch) Used to determine the resolution of a digital image, this is the number of dots per inch within a given image's dot matrix.

Dye-sublimation Printing There are two forms of this kind of printing – indirect and direct. In the indirect method an image is first printed onto paper using disperse dyes. By means of a heat press, the dye particles are then changed into gas, and so transferred onto polyester-based fabric. In the direct method, the image is printed onto the fabric substrate, then fixed using heat.

E

Eco Design A method of designing a product that takes into account its impact on the environment at all stages of its life cycle.

Electrostatic Printing Also known as laser printing. A process where liquid toner is adhered to a light-sensitive print drum, static electricity is then used to transfer the toner onto the printing medium to which it is fused via heat and pressure. This is the technology used in most photocopiers.

Emulsion A mixture of two unblendable substances; light-sensitive emulsions are often used in the preparation of hand silk screens.

Engraver In the textile industry this refers to a company who prepare silk screens for printing.

Engraving In the textile industry this term refers to the process of preparing a silk screen.

Engineered Print (also known as a placement print) A print where the design is laid out to fit the pattern pieces and structure of a garment.

F

Fixation The process of permanently bonding a dye or pigment to a substrate.

Fixation Agent (also known as a mordant) The chemicals used to aid the process of permanently bonding a pigment or dye to a substrate.

Flat Bed Silk Screen A silk screen that is stretched over a rectangular frame.

Flock Printing A method where areas of the fabric are first printed with glue, and then have flock fibres or paper applied to them. Once dried, the excess flock is removed to leave a raised velvet-like surface.

G

Gravure Printing A printing process where the image to be printed is engraved into a metal plate.

H

Halftone In the context of digital printing, a word that is used to describe the shade of a colour as it gradates from dark to light in an image such as a watercolour.

Heat Photogram A method of printing where dyes are painted onto transfer paper, an object is then impressed directly onto the paper to create a design, and heat is used to transfer the image onto fabric.

I

ICC The International Colour Consortium. An organization that creates objective standards for defining and communicating colour.

ICC Profile A set of data defined by the ICC that characterizes a colour input or output device, or a colour space.

Inkjet Printing A specific form of digital printing that works by propelling variably sized droplets of liquid, or molten ink, onto the substrate. The two main types of inkjet printing technology are DOD (drop on demand) and continuous flow. (See also Continuous Flow Inkjet Technology and DOD.)

J

Jpeg (Joint Photographic Expert Group) A popular file format for compressing and saving digitized photographs and images.

L

Laminating A process of using heat or pressure to bond two or more materials, such as plastic and fabric, often used to make waterproof fabric.

Large Format Printer Term used to describe all printers that are wider than desk-top printers, and that are usually designed to accommodate rolls of material and print longer lengths.

Lay Plan A grouping of pattern pieces as they are laid out on a piece of cloth before cutting.

Light Box A specialist piece of equipment used in the colour matching process to view colours under a set of standardized light sources, such as simulated daylight or UV light.

M

Mass Customization A term used to describe the semi-customization of products where the customer is able to personalize an item by choosing from a pre-set number of features.

Micro-encapsulation A process in which tiny particles or droplets are surrounded by a coating.

Moiré Pattern A pattern where the design or texture of a fabric creates a wave-like effect.

Monochrome An image whose range of colours is made of shades of a single hue, usually black.

P

Photochemical Process A process that involves the chemical action of light. Within the context of this book it refers to a technique where a light-sensitive substance is used to transfer an image or photograph onto a substrate.

Photomontage A technique of producing a composite image by combining a series of photographs.

Piezoelectricity Electricity (or electric polarity, produced by the piezoelectric effect) by which some materials such as crystals and certain ceramics generate an electric potential in response to applied mechanical stress. As opposed to thermal DOD, this is the primary technology used to create the ink drops in piezoelectric DOD inkjet printing.

Pigment A substance that imparts colour to other materials. Unlike dyes, pigments are not designed to permeate the fabric of the substrate, and bond only to its surface.

Pixel The smallest and most basic unit of visual information for a digitized image.

Polymer A large synthetic molecule composed of repeating structural units, usually of high molecular weight. An example of a polymer-based fabric is polyester.

Primary Colours Basic colours from which all other colours can be made. In the context of this book, the primary colours are those associated with the CMYK and RGB systems. (See also CMYK and RGB.)

Print Head The part of the printer that contains the print nozzles that are responsible for firing the ink droplets at the substrate during printing.

Prototype The original or model on which a product design is based or formed.

R

Raster A raster graphics image or bitmap is a data structure representing a generally rectangular grid of pixels, or points of color, as opposed to a vector-based image that is based on geometry.

Rasterize To convert an image into a matrix of pixels. (See also RIP.)

RGB An additive colour model comprised of three basic colours – red, green and blue – emitted as light and combined to create a broad array of colours. Digital cameras, computer monitors and television all use the RGB system as opposed to the CMYK system used in digital printing, in which the pigments are not emitted as light, but as ink to be absorbed by the substrate. (See also CMYK.)

Ready-to-wear The garments in a fashion designer's collection that are produced in large enough quantities so that they may be marketed widely as opposed to limited editions, couture and show pieces. (Also known as prêt a porter.)

Repeat A method of laying out/repeating an image unit to create a continuous pattern.

Reprographic The reproduction of text and images through mechanical or electrical means, such as photography and offset printing.

Resolution Term used to measure the level of detail in a digital image. Resolution is determined by the dpi (dots per inch) within a given digital image's dot matrix. (See also dpi.)

RIP (Raster Image Processor) Software used in printing that converts an RGB image into the pixel-based CMYK data needed to drive the printer.

Rotary Screen Printing A form of mechanized silk screen printing where the screen is a cylinder.

S

Scan The process of capturing the 2D or 3D data of an image or object such as a fabric, photograph or drawing into a digital image (see also body scanner).

Shibori Collective term for the different resist-based techniques of tie–dye, stitch-dye, fold-dye and pole-wrap-dye. (See also batik.)

Silk Screen A method of printing where a fabric with fine, porous mesh (often silk) is stretched over a frame. The design is then delineated by masking out the areas of the design that will not be printed, leaving areas open for each colour, through which the ink is pushed using a squeegee.

Spectrophotometer A device for measuring light intensity as it relates to the colour of the light.

Spot Colour In printing, a term for any ink other than one of the four CMYK colours (cyan, magenta, yellow and black).

Steamer In the context of this book, the term is used to describe a device that generates steam at high temperatures and is used to fix dyes after printing.

Stencil A technique for printing where holes defining the shape to be printed are cut into a thin material, such as a metal sheet or waxed paper, through which the colourant is then pushed.

Substrate In the context of this book, the term for any material which forms the printing surface.

Sublimation The transference of a substance from a solid to a gaseous state without passing through a liquid stage.

Strike-off An industry term used to describe a test sample meant to indicate what a design will look like once put into production.

T

Thermochromic A substance that changes colour in relation to temperature.

Tiff (Tagged Image File Format) A popular format for saving digitized photographs and images.

Toile In the context of this book the term refers to a trial version or prototype of a garment.

U

Upcycling The practice of taking something that is disposable and transforming it into something of greater use and value.

V

Vector Graphic A digitized drawing that is based on lines and geometry rather than the individual pixels in raster-based programs, thus allowing it to be manipulated and scaled without affecting its image resolution.

W

Woodblock A carved block used to transfer a design onto fabric.

DIGITAL PRINT BUREAUS

UK
Artisan: tel: 0044 (0) 1625 869859
CAD Works UK Ltd (Pigment printing only):
  www.cadworksuk.co.uk
Cameron Gillmartin: www.camerongilmartin.co.uk
Centre for Advanced Textiles: www.catdigital.co.uk
Cloth: www.clothuk.com
Colplan Engineering Ltd: 0044 (0) 1706 655899
Digetex: www.digetex.com
Digital Fashion Print, London College of Fashion:
  www.fashion.arts.ac.uk
Direct Textile Imaging Ltd (Heat transfer printing):
  Tel: 0044 (0)1706 656070
Elanbach: www.elanbach.com
FabPad: www.fabricprint.co.uk
Forest Digital: www.forestdigital.co.uk
RA Smart Ltd: www.rasmart.co.uk
The Silk Bureau: www.silkbureau.co.uk

USA
Advanced Digital Textiles:
  www.advdigitaltextiles.com
Carlisle Finishing LLC: www.itg-global.com
Custom Fabric Printing:
  www.customprintedfabrics.com
Dream Digital Fabric Printing Services
  www.dreamfabricprinting.com
Dye-Namix: www.dyenamix.com
Fabrics2Dye4, LLC: www.fabrics2dye4.com
First2Print: www.first2print.com
LTS Design: www.ltsdesign.net
ROTHTEC Engraving Corporation:
  www.rothtec.com
The Style Council: www.stylecouncil.com
Supersample: www.supersample.com

DIGITAL PRINTER SUPPLIERS
AVA: www.avacadcam.com (international)
Digifab: www.digifab.com (USA)
ITNH: www.itnh.com (USA)
Jacquard Inkjet Fabric Systems:
  www.inkjetfabrics.com (USA)
Sawgrass: www.sawgrassink.com (international)
Stork: www.storkprints.com (international)
RA Smart Ltd: www.rasmart.co.uk (UK)

SOFTWARE MANUFACTURERS
Adobe software (design): www.adobe.com
Aleph (design, colour management, RIP):
  www.alephteam.com
AVA (design, colour management, RIP):
  www.avacadcam.com
Clickdesign (design): www.clicdesign.com
EAT (design): www.designscopecompany.com
Ergo Soft (colour management, RIP):
  www.ergosoft.ch
Lectra (design, colour management, RIP):
  www.lectra.com
NedGraphics (design, colour management, RIP):
  www.nedgraphics.com
Pointcarré (design, colour management, RIP):
  www.pointcarre.com
Scotweave (design): www.scotweave.com
Shiraz (colour management): www.uscgp.com
Stork (colour management, RIP):
  www.storktextile.com
Wasatch (colour management):
  www.wasatch.com
Yxendis (design): www.yxendis.com

COLOUR MANAGEMENT HARDWARE
X-Rite: www.usa.gretagmacbethstore.com

FABRIC AND INK SUPPLIERS

UK
AVA (ink): www.avacadcam.com
Colplan Engineering Ltd (ink):
  tel: 0044 (0) 1706 655899
RA Smart Ltd (ink and fabric):
  www.rasmart.co.uk
Target Transfers (CAD/CUT materials):
  www.targettransfer.com
Whaleys of Bradford (fabric):
  www.whaleys.co.uk

USA
AVA (ink): www.avacadcam.com
Digifab (fabric): www.digifab.com
Fisher (fabric): www.fishertextiles.com
Jacquard Inkjet Fabric Systems (ink and fabric):
  www.inkjetfabrics.com
Stork (ink): www.storkprints.com

FURTHER READING
Adobe Creative Team, *Adobe Illustrator CS3: Classroom in a Book,* Adobe, 2007

Adobe Creative Team, *Adobe Photoshop CS3: Classroom in a Book*, Adobe, 2007

Blackley, Lachlan, *Wallpaper*, Laurence King Publishing, 2006

Borrelli, Laird, *Fashion Illustration by Fashion Designers,* Thames & Hudson, 2008

Borrelli, Laird, *Fashion Illustration Next*, Thames & Hudson, 2004

Braddock Clarke, Sarah E and Marie O'Mahony, *Techno Textiles 2: Revolutionary Fabrics for Fashion and Design*, Thames & Hudson, 2005

Brittain-Catlin, Timothy, Jane Audas and Charles Stuckey, *The Cutting Edge of Wallpaper*, Black Dog Publishing, 2006

Colchester, Chloë, *Textiles Today,* Thames & Hudson, 2009

Cole, Drusilla, *Patterns*, Laurence King Publishing, 2008

Colussy, Kathleen M and Steve Greenberg, *Rendering Fashion, Fabric & Prints With Adobe Illustrator*, Prentice Hall, 2006

Da Cruz, Elyssa and Sandy Black, *Fashioning Fabrics: Contemporary Textiles in Fashion*, Black Dog Publishing, 2006

Fish, June, *Designing and Printing Textiles*, The Crowood Press, 2005

Fogg, Marnie, *Print in Fashion*, Batsford, 2009
Jenkyn Jones, Sue, *Fashion Design: 2nd edition*, Laurence King Publishing, 2005

Udale, Jenny, *Textiles and Fashion*, AVA, 2008

Ujiie, Hitoshi (ed.), *Digital Printing of Textiles*, Woodhead Publishing, 2006

Vilaseca, Estel, *Cutting Edge Patterns and Texture*, Rockport, 2008

USEFUL INFORMATION
American Association of Textile Chemists & Colorists: www.aatcc.org

Melanie Bowles, Senior Lecturer in Digital Textiles, Chelsea College of Art and Design: www.melaniebowles.co.uk

Computer Arts: monthly publication: www.computerarts.co.uk

Digital Stylist (news, software updates and tutorials in digital design): www.thedigitalstylist.com

Digital Textile (textile industry news website): www.inteletex.com

The Dover Bookshop (copyright-free books and images): www.doverbooks.co.uk

Prof Hitoshi Ujiie, The Center for Excellence of Digital Inket Printing of Textiles: www.hitoshiujiie.com

Ceri Isaac, Research Fellow, The Centre for Fashion Science, London College of Fashion: www.fashion.arts.ac.uk/lcf-research.htm

SDC Society for Dyers & Colourists: www.sdc.org.uk

TC2 (non-profit organization that provides information and undertakes research into emerging technologies within the industry): www.tc2.com

TECHEXCHANGE (online trade publication and sourcing portal for technology solutions for the textile industry): www.techexchange.com

TED (Textile Environmental Design): www.tedresearch.net

TRFG (Textile Futures Research Group): www.tfrg.org.uk

Web Consulting (industry info and market analysis): www.web-na.com

TRADE SHOWS
CITDA (American Association of Textile Chemists and Colourists): www.aatcc.org

FESPA (Federation of European Screenprinters Associations, organizer of the world's leading screenprinting and digital imaging exhibitions): www.fespa.com

ITMA (The worlds largest International Exhibition of Textile Machinery): www.itma.com

Protextiledigital (European Digital Textile Show): www.english.protextiledigital.com

CREDITS

PHOTO CREDITS

The authors and publisher would like to thank the following for providing images for use in this book. In all cases, every effort has been made to credit the copyright holders, but should there be any omissions or errors the publisher would be pleased to insert the appropriate acknowledgment in any subsequent edition of this book. Where credit has been given in the caption within the book, it is not repeated here.

Photography of student work throughout: Melanie Bowles, Rebecca Earley and Kenny Taylor
p4 design by Photini Anastasi
p6 design by Kitty Joseph
p8 'Pink Jellyfish' design by Sarah Arnett
p10 Football bag print © Paul Smith
p11 Basso & Brooke © firstVIEW; Sarah Easom courtesy Cameron Gilmartin
p12 Jonathon Saunders © firstVIEW; Giles Deacon courtesy of the designer; Basso & Brooke © firstVIEW
p13 Jean Paul Gaultier © firstVIEW; Ralph Rucci courtesy Patricia Mears
p14 Paul Smith © firstVIEW; Showroom dummies courtesy of the designer
p16 Win Sei Yau © catwalking.com; Hussein Chalayan © catwalking.com; Lucinda Abell, photography Vivien Fettke
p17 Comme des Garçons © firstVIEW
p19 Hussein Chalayan © firstVIEW; Alexander McQueen © firstVIEW
p20 Avatar software by Opitex
p21 Hussein Chalayan courtesy of the designer
p22 design by Melanie Bowles
p24 Ross Barnes © catwalking.com
p81 Westside Story © Getty Images
p86 design by Kenny Taylor
p120 illustration by Chae Young Kim
p140 design by Melanie Bowles
p149 Matthew Williamson © firstVIEW
p166 design by Win Sei Yau
p168 Joyce Clissold courtesy the Museum and Contemporary Collection, Central Saint Martins
p169 'Toile de Jouy' print courtesy V&A Museum
p170 Flatbed screen printer courtesy Magnoprint; rotary screen printer courtesy Stork Prints BV; Paul Smith courtesy of the designer
p171 'Hobie' shirt courtesy Benny's Aloha Shirts, CA
p172 illustration by Advanced Illustration Ltd
p178 Mimaki printer courtesy RA Smart; ISIS printer courtesy OSIRIS Digital Prints BV
p180 images courtesy AVA
p181 images courtesy AVA
p183 colour space image courtesy AVA; colour matching image courtesy Nick Cicconi at John Kaldor UK Ltd.
p184 images courtesy of Ratti Spa
p186 flexible screen courtesy Universal Display Corporation; Hussein Chalayan © catwalking.com; LED sofa courtesy Philips

PUBLISHER'S ACKNOWLEDGMENTS

The publisher would like to thank the following:
Anita Racine, Department of Textiles and Apparel, Cornell University
Edward J Herczyk, School of Engineering and Textiles, Philadelphia University
Philippa Brock, School of Fashion & Textiles, CSM, University of the Arts, London
Marcy L Koontz, Department of Clothing, Textiles and Interior Design, University of Alabama

AUTHORS' ACKNOWLEDGMENTS

We would like to thank all the designers, students, organizations and individuals whose contributions and support have made this book possible. Their shared enthusiasm for the subject matter has been a revelation.

Special thanks are due to:
Hitoshi Ujiie, Amanda Briggs, AVA and our editors Gaynor Sermon and Anne Townley at Laurence King Publishing. Thanks also to Melanie Mues for her wonderful design of the book. Invaluable support was given by the research departments, staff and students at Chelsea College of Art and Design as well as The London College of Fashion. The project was aided by funding from The University of the Arts, London and CLIP/CETL (Creative Learning in Practice Centre for Excellence in Teaching and Learning).

We are also most grateful to:
Kenny Taylor, Kathryn Round, Jemima Gregson, Claire Thorpe, Andrea Patterson, Emamoke Ukeleghe, Katie Irving Jones, Hong Yeon Yun, Chae Young Kim, Daisy Butler, Katie Hoppe, Jane Walker, and Alex Madjitey, who generously assisted in the development of the design tutorials.

Last but not least heartfelt thanks belong to:
Philip Dolman, Ben, Eve and Maya Dolman-Bowles, Barbara Isaac, and all our friends and family who have lent their encouragement along the way.

We would also like to extend our thanks to the following companies and individuals:
Lucinda Abell, aforest-design, Dorte Agergaard, Photini Anastasi, Sarah Arnett, Charlotte Arnold, Toluwalope Ashiru, Alexa Ball, Zoe Barker, Ross Barnes, Brian Barrett, Lisa Batchelor, Steven Bateman at The Museum and Contemporary Collection at CSM, Patricia Belford, Benny's Aloha Shirts, Sandy Black, Petra Boase, Rachel Boxall, Amy Isla Breckon, Helena Britt, Nicolette Brunklaus, Clare Cameron and Jacqui Gilmartin at Cameron Gilmartin, Margaret Campbell, Claire Canning, The Centre for Fashion Science at LCF, Hussein Chalayan, Kim Chin, Nick Cicconi at John Kaldor UK Ltd, Clothuk, Victoria Collins, Jennifer Cooper, Maria Da luz Andrade, Dominique Devaux, The Digital Fashion Print Bureau at LCF, Rebecca Earley, Sarah Easom, Elanbach, Louise–Claire Fernandes, Pauline Fernandez, First2Print, Nicky Gearing, Shelly Goldsmith, Joanna Green, Zoe Harrington, Nada Herceg, Emily House, Dingus Hussey, Kitty Joseph, Helen Kemp, Taina Lehtinen, Rosie MacCurrach, Charlotte Mann, Lara Mantell , Amelia Mullins, Vicki Murdoch, Helen Amy Murray, Osiris Digital Prints BV, Georgina Papandreou, Philips, Gina Pierce, Professor Kay Politowicz, Alice Potter, Chetna Prajapti, Victoria Purver, RA Smart, Emma Rampton, Ratti Spa, Kathryn Round, Ralph Rucci, Dani Salvadori, Showroom Dummies, Sir Paul Smith, Debbie Stack, Emma Stone, Stork Prints BV, Target Transfers, Timorous Beasties, Louise Townsend, Joan Truckenbrod, Claire Turner, Heather Ujiie, The Universal Display Company, The V&A Museum, Wexla, Stacey Wickens, Win Sei Yau, Zimmer Textile Technology, Leanna Zivanovic.